Princess of the Mary Rose

by

JAMES GAINEY

Angel Press

First published by
Angel Press, PO Box 60, East Wittering, West Sussex 1986

British Library Catalogue in Publication Data
Gainey, James
Princess of the Mary Rose
    1. Mary, *Queen consort Louis XII, King of France*
    2. France - Queen - Bibliography. 3. Mary Rose (ship)
    4. Great Britain - History, Naval - Tudors, 1485-1603
    I. Title
944'. 027'09924 Dc109

ISBN 0-947785-16-7

Typeset in England by Castle Printers of Wittering
Printed and Bound by
Caligraving Limited Thetford, Norfolk England

To Vanna

Foreword

Many readers, like myself, will have been fascinated by the raising of the warship *MARY ROSE* but how many of us know much about the princess after whom it was named.

I read this book with great interest and enjoyed it, recognising the thoroughness of the research by the author, although not agreeing with all his personal thoughts or conclusions on the royal Tudors.

As a descendant of the princess, I wish the book well and hope it will encourage interest in our history, interest in the *MARY ROSE* and be of help to the Mary Rose Trust.

The Countess of Loudoun

Introduction

This book tells the story of a lovely princess who became a queen, and of a great warship which was named after her. Both had short lives in a turbulent period of English history - the reign of Henry VIII.

The story of the ship has become part of today's news - that of the princess is less well known, and I was particularly interested to read it as I am descended, mainly in the female line, from her. One of my ancestors, who bore the same name as myself, was one of the many knights who attended her funeral at St Edmundsbury Abbey in Suffolk.

What a fascinating character she must have been! Well known throughout Europe for her great beauty, she had also great charm and great determination. She was like her brother King Henry VIII in this, although unlike him in her staunch loyalty to her friends.

Hitherto so little has been told about her that the appearance of this book is a welcome event, and the linking of her story with that of the now resurrected ship brings her dramatically to life.

The book was born from the publicity given to the raising of the warship and it is to be hoped that it will arouse some interest in romantic history in the present generation.

Sir Edmund Bedingfeld

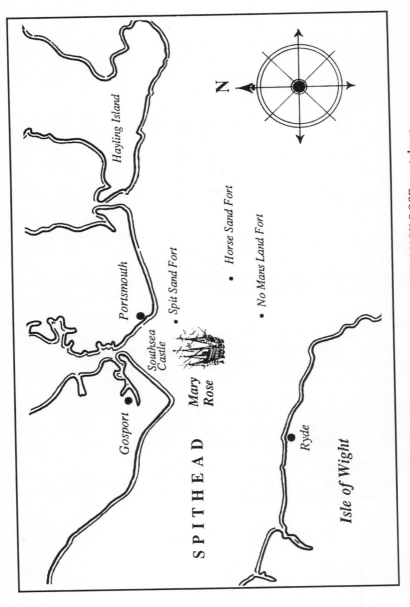

The Solent, showing the site where the *MARY ROSE* went down.

Princess Mary Tudor and Charles Brandon, Duke of Suffolk

King Louis XII of France

Chapter One

The union of King Henry VII and Princess Elizabeth of York in January 1486 was welcomed with great joy by the nobility, clergy and common people of England, as it heralded the end of the terrible Civil War known as the Wars of the Roses which had long devastated the countryside and spilt so much blood. Country folk had seen their crops destroyed, their men press-ganged into rival armies, their children suffer hunger - not infrequently death - from starvation.

The nobles often changed sides but this did not save their lives, for most of the great families had relatives whose heads had been separated from their shoulders. Royalty was not spared. Persons of the Blood Royal had been murdered and tortured in the most frightful ways - often in the Tower of London. Even young children had been victims in the struggle for the golden circle that is the symbol of kingship.

Henry was a Lancastrian and Elizabeth a Yorkist. The ravaged country saw in their marriage something which would heal wounds and be a lasting cause of unity and an end of strife. And so it proved to be. Their children were neither Lancastrian nor Yorkist - only English. As a token of this new found unity, the White Rose and the Red Rose were joined together to make the badge of the new Tudor dynasty - a rose with alternate white and red petals: a double flower. This marriage was exactly what the nation needed, for peace immediately reigned throughout England, except for a few small revolts which were easily put down.

The issue of this union of many pregnancies:
1. Arthur, Prince of Wales. Born 1486. Married Katherine, Princess of Aragon in 1501. A delicate young man who was not able to consummate marriage. He died in 1502.
2. Princess Margaret. Born 1489. Later Queen and, still

later, Queen Mother and Regent of Scotland. Married James IV in 1503. Plain of face and squat of figure, she led a most wretched life in the unhappy quarrelsome land of Scotland amid an almost permanent Civil War. She lived through incredible adventures to die in 1541. We hear more of her later in this book.

3. Henry, Duke of York. Later Henry VIII. Born 1491. Married his widowed sister-in-law, Katherine of Aragon, Princess of Wales, in 1509. In youth a popular prince and monarch, he had enormous physical strength and was remarkably handsome, with charming manners and a happy smile. He was a great horseman, hunter and tennis player. He loved rich clothes and fabulous jewelry. He had no idea of managing money and was a spendthrift all his life. A first-class lutist, he also composed. He had a strong accurate voice. He was a linguist, an intellectual, no mean poet. A religious man, he was to begin with a faithful son of the Catholic Church. The other side of the coin showed him to be a bold womaniser who was kind to a discarded mistress by marrying her off to a courtier and thus ensuring her future. Later in life his character changed as a result of an obsession to sire a male heir. He became irritable, bad-tempered, cruel, vindictive, greedy with food and drink. He sent his subjects to the block after frightful tortures for the slightest adverse criticism. His victims included statesmen and clergy. He cut off the heads of two wives and a third just escaped a similar fate by his death.

4. Elizabeth. Born 1492. Died 1495.

5. Mary. Born 1496. Later Queen of France. Still later Duchess of Suffolk. All her life she was greatly loved at the English and French courts. Her father was indulgent and spoilt her, no doubt because of her outstanding beauty and pretty ways. Her royal brother adored her and was loved by her in return. This mutual feeling lasted until King Henry repudiated his queen and married Anne Boleyn - her former Maid of Honour. Then a coldness came between them and her brother's resentment pursued her even after her death in 1533.

6. Edmund. Born 1500. Died 1501.

7. Katherine. Born 1503. Died 1503.

In accordance with royal custom, the Princess Mary from the age of three had her own household. It comprised her much loved governess, Lady Guildford, several teachers, ladies-in-waiting, a doctor and, of course, several male and female servants. She had a quick brain and learned French and Latin. When quite small, she played a miniature lute on which she accompanied herself when singing childish songs in a tiny sweet voice. Rapidly becoming skilled in the complicated steps of court dances, she gave her parents great amusement by performing before the court. Dressed as a miniature adult, with rigid head-dress and stiff wide skirts to the floor, she always wore a quantity of necklaces, bracelets and rings made specially for her.

A very affectionate child, she was particularly close to Prince Henry and her governess Lady Guildford, and her youthful life could be described as happy. She enjoyed the frequent trips made with her sister and brothers between the palaces of Sheen, Windsor, Richmond, Westminster, Baynard's Castle, the Tower, Greenwich and Eltham in large royal barges painted in the Queen's colours of green and white. Often a lutist - with perhaps a singer - amused the children on the journey.

The little princess had a fragile and delicate beauty which she inherited from her mother. She had a great quantity of fair fine hair, gold in colour with a reddish tinge. Her eyes were a wonderful blue. Few details of her early childhood survive, but one inventory of her possessions records that she and her large household were well provided with furniture, bed linen, carpets, clothes and tableware.

In 1498, Henry VII received the first offer of a political marriage for his infant daughter Mary. It came from the Duke Ludovico Sforza of Milan who at that time was threatened by several potential enemies, including France. As bridegroom, he proposed his son the Count of Pavia. However, Henry refused the offer, as France and England happened to be at peace, and also because he had only just made the French king a Knight of the Garter.

At the turn of the century, the Palace of Sheen was destroyed by fire and not for the first time. It was a much loved residence of Henry VII and he ordered it to be rebuilt. His young children also enjoyed staying there - more for the outdoor activities than for the mansion itself. The hunting was first class and the tilt-yard was famous as were the extensive formal Tudor gardens.

Sir Thomas More and the philosopher Erasmus visited the Palace of Eltham in 1499 to talk to the royal children. Both were outstanding intellectuals, and Henry and Margaret chatted to the famous visitors while Mary played with some games on the floor. More exclaimed to attendants on the remarkable

11

childish beauty of the infant Mary and indeed mentioned this in a description he wrote of the meeting.

Queen Elizabeth did not over-indulge her daughters, although she made sure they had a full wardrobe of rich clothes, dress ornaments and jewelry. She was a good mother in the style of the period for royalty, and a generous alms giver. She even economised in her personal expenses so that she could help her favourite charities. Henry VII had the deserved reputation of being a miser and greedy, but he did not begrudge the large sums spent on costly pomp and ceremony.

State duties kept the queen busy and away from her children many times a year and then often their grandmother, Margaret Beaufort, Countess of Richmond, came to keep them company. The countess was very rich and a wonderful mediaeval character: she was patron of the arts and endowed several convents and colleges of learning, at least one of her foundations existing to this day. Her favourite, Mary, received many presents from her and was specially remembered in her will.

The sovereigns took enormous pleasure in the marriage of Arthur, Prince of Wales to the Princess Katherine of Aragon. Both bride and bridegroom were only fifteen. He was shy and not robust of health. She was desperately anxious to please but she spoke no English, knew nothing of English customs and had been used to a very sheltered life at a very formal court in Andalucia. They were just two rather frightened children.

The younger members of the Royal Family were wild with excitement, for a wedding meant new clothes, presents and lots of fun. Mary was just five in 1501, but quickly made friends with Katherine - a friendship that was to prove lifelong. Prince Henry danced every dance, mostly with his sister Margaret. All this energy made him so hot that he discarded his long gown and raised court eyebrows as he chose to remain in shirt sleeves. As for Mary, she wore a velvet dress with a silk kirtle of green. The Countess of Richmond wept throughout the Nuptial Mass of her grandson.

St Paul's Cathedral in London was the setting for the ceremony. The bridal dress included a Spanish mantilla which partly hid the face. Katherine did not wish her bridegroom to see her unveiled before he met her in church, but her royal father-in-law insisted that she uncover when he first met her on the Chertsey to Portsmouth road and after consulting the Privy Council. On her arrival in London, the court was astonished to see the princess wearing a broad round red hat rather like a cardinal's tied with golden lace. Great interest was also aroused at the very stiff farthingale she wore, as that fashion had not before been seen in England.

Londoners gave the young Spanish princess a right royal welcome as she passed through the streets, which pleased her greatly and to which she responded with graceful gestures.

After the wedding, Arthur endowed the princess with a third of his property and presented her with a large casket of magnificent jewelry. The newlyweds went to live at Baynard's Castle (near the Tower) with Queen Elizabeth during the several days of festivities appropriate to the nuptials of the heir to the throne. The jousting went on for hours, Katherine presenting the prizes to winners. The daily state banquets of many courses had to be endured, but these were enlivened by a kind of cabaret-cum-circus with clowns, jesters, singers, dancers and acrobats.

The king decreed that the young couple should take up residence at Ludlow Castle in Shropshire. They set out to travel in easy stages. The new Princess of Wales rode pillion behind her Master of the Horse, but when tired, she took to her horse litter. The king's plan was that Arthur should govern the Principality of Wales, and to this end the young prince established a small court on arrival.

After only five months of marriage, Prince Arthur, continuously in poor health, caught an illness (not known but contagious) and died quickly. Princess Katherine was left almost penniless for she had not received her wedding portion, and her prince had left everything he had to his elder sister Margaret. The marriage had not been consummated, so the unfortunate Katherine was not married and therefore could not be a widow. Nevertheless she carried the title of Dowager Princess of Wales.

Queen Elizabeth was at Greenwich Palace when she learned of her sixteen-year-old son's death. Completely shattered, she showed her grief so openly that she became hysterical: weeping, screaming, throwing herself about the room. Her attendants held her down fearing for her sanity. Even in her sorrow she thought of the poor foreign princess alone at Ludlow and in pity sent a litter for her to establish her in residence at Croydon Palace. Elizabeth took a continued maternal interest in her daughter-in-law and constantly showed her many acts of kindness.

For Mary, the court mourning for the Prince of Wales was soon relieved by arrangements for the proxy wedding of her sister Margaret, aged thirteen, to the King of Scotland, James IV, the negotiations for which had dragged on since 1495. The

13

Papal Dispensation had only just come to hand (the couple were within the prohibited degrees of relationship). The ceremony was held at Richmond and afterwards there was much rejoicing together with jousting. The proxy marriage was very expensive but King Henry did not hesitate to dip into the treasury on this occasion. Being thirteen, Margaret was not to be allowed to go to Scotland for another year.

The queen's health at this time was very poor, probably because of several difficult pregnancies. She made pilgrimages to different shrines of Our Lady to beg for strength, at the same time giving large sums in alms to the poor and destitute. Pregnant again, she became restless and travelled by litter and barge from palace to palace, hardly knowing what she wanted or where she was going. As usual, Elizabeth was heavily in debt, which made her parsimonious husband very angry. She was not a lover of luxury and disliked extravagance but she always found it difficult to resist the call of the suffering. She had already pawned much of her plate and jewelry so, untypically, Henry made her a present of a large sum to tide her over her difficulties.

Still unsettled in her mind, she aimlessly took her state barge up and down the river from Greenwich to Richmond reclining on cushions and listening to a minstrel playing the lute and singing those sad little love songs so favoured in that period.

Unaccountably, Elizabeth chose to lie in at the Tower, that dreadful palace of ill omen, where so much blood of her own family had been spilt and where her two small brothers had been smothered by pillows to be buried nobody knew where. By an oversight, her gynaecologist, Dr Hallyswurth, had not been commanded to attend at the Tower and was still at his Kentish home. He was sent for as soon as labour began and left his house immediately, galloping on good horses throughout the night, escorted by guides carrying torches. But he came to the mother's bedside only to find that she had died - and on her thirty-seventh birthday. Her sister, Lady Katherine Courtenay, who was experienced as a midwife, had done her best. The baby, Princess Katherine, lived only a few hours. So little Katherine shared with her mother a funeral and a grave in Westminster Abbey.

The king rode in haste to the Tower in a state of shock. After gazing briefly at the bodies of his wife and child, he broke down in a storm of weeping, unable to speak. Beckoning a few servants, he rode to a secret place to pray and give full rein to his great sorrow.

Elizabeth of York, like so many persons near to the throne in mediaeval times had undergone close imprisonment in dark and cold castles and many were the occasions when she was in real danger of assassination or execution. More than anyone else she had cause to welcome the cessation of the Wars of the Roses. She enjoyed to the full the peace and prosperity her husband's reign had brought.

She was a kind and gentle lady and a good mother within the limits of royal custom, which prescribed that infants should live apart from their parents with separate households and domestic staff.

Elizabeth could not bear to refuse charity to someone she heard was in trouble. She really loved music, and became the patroness of many young musicians and singers. She publicly showed her love for her husband and he loved her too, in a quiet way, for he was not demonstrative. He was never known to have been unfaithful.

Henry honoured his queen in the only way he knew, by giving her a magnificent funeral and a grand tomb. Bells tolled continuously from every church, convent and monastery in London during the twelve days of the lying-in-state, when the queen's corpse, embalmed and in a lead coffin, was watched by gentlemen of her household. Then from the black draped chapel in the Tower, the bodies of mother and baby were placed on an open hearse which, following custom, also carried an effigy of Elizabeth in full regalia.

Her maids of honour in mourning dress rode on palfreys with black saddle cloths, and all the way from the Tower to the Abbey in each doorway stood a person in black with bowed head, a lighted torch in hand. Standing in Cheapside was a group of thirty-seven virgins with lighted tapers (one maiden for each year of the queen's age). The procession was endless and included monks and nuns from every religious house in the capital and nearby: most of them had been at one time or another beneficiaries of the royal bounty.

The next morning, Requiem Mass was sung, attended by the widower king and Elizabeth's surviving children: Princess Margaret (14), Henry, Duke of York (12) and Princess Mary (7). Kneeling together by the coffin, Henry held his sister's hand.

As the remains were lowered into the tomb, the Bishop of Rochester preached a sermon on the text - very popular at funerals - "Have pity, have pity on me, my friends, for the hand of God has touched me." The Tomb and effigy (counted as a great work of art) was sculpted by Torregiano who did

15

most of his work for Lorenzo de Medici in Florence.
Her (Latin) inscription can clearly be read today -

> Here rests Queen Elizabeth, daughter of Edward IV,
> sometime monarch of this realm, sister of Edward V who
> bore the title of king, wedded to King Henry VII, the
> illustrious mother of Henry VIII, who closed her life in the
> palace of the Tower of London on 11th February 1503
> having completed her 37th year.

Henry had not begrudged the money spent on building the
magnificent Henry VII chapel in the abbey for the resting places
of himself and his family.

Sir Thomas More wrote a poem of lamentation for the
death of his queen:

> Adieu, Lord Henry, loving son, adieu,
> Our Lord increase your honour and estate.
> Adieu my daughter Mary, bright of hue,
> God make you virtuous, wise and fortunate.
> Adieu, sweetheart my little daughter Kate:
> Thou shalt, sweet babe - such is my destiny -
> Thy mother never know, for here I lie.[1]

On the death of her mother, the bewildered Princess Mary
was sent to live with the sixteen-year-old widow Katherine,
Dowager Princess of Wales, at Durham House on the Strand,
London. The two at once became friends and a happy family
life was soon organised by Lady Guildford, Mary's adored
governess. Both princesses looked back on this time in their
lives with great affection, for it was peaceful - a rarity for
royalty. This truly happy period was only marred by Henry
VII's avarice, for he kept Katherine completely without money
so that she was not able to pay her servants, which was very
worrying. She had no means at all of paying her debts, so she
wrote many pleading letters to her father for money. She asked
the king for permission to return to Spain, but he would not
permit this as he wanted her rich dowry to remain in England,
thinking that she might well make a bride for his second son
Henry. When this possibility was put to her Katherine sent a
flood of letters to Spain begging her father not to agree to this,
for she disliked intensely the idea of a second marriage in
England.

This kind of persecution had been going on ever since the
death of Arthur, Prince of Wales in 1502, and it continued until

the king's own death. It was entirely due to Henry's obsession with money. His greed grew over the years and became worse after his queen's death. Always something of a miser, he was ever ready to raise taxes which was loudly resented by his already heavily burdened subjects.

Puberty now having arrived for the Princess Margaret, it was arranged that the fourteen-year-old bride should set out for Edinburgh to join James IV, the husband she had been married to by proxy the year before. The poor child was to suffer much there and make many political mistakes. Her journey north took two months of almost continuous festivities: High Masses, banquets, processions, public receptions, presentations of notables. For these she was always dressed in elaborate costumes and head-dresses weighted down by heavy jewelry. Unusually, Henry VII spent a large sum on equipping his daughter to show that she was important to England and so to inspire respect in James and his court.

Margaret's departure was accepted as inevitable by herself and her brother, Henry, the Duke of York. It was Mary who shed many tears and suffered much sadness after she had been told by a courtier that she would never see her sister again. Not quite accurate as it turned out.

During mediaeval times, England had expended all her national resources on fighting in France to retain lands she reckoned to be legitimately hers - territory conquered by force of arms or brought as the marriage settlement of a French royal bride. Almost every queen of England had been French for five centuries, but the area controlled by England did not remain constant. With every invasion, with every battle, the frontiers changed, until in the fifteenth century, at long last England seemed to begin to realise that the struggle was futile and a waste of money and men. By the reign of Henry VII, English possessions in France had shrunk to the enclave of Calais.

It became apparent to the English king that ships (hitherto used almost solely as troop transports for France) should now be heavily armed with cannon and equipped expressly as naval fighting ships. They could then be used for raiding French ports and for keeping the Channel open, as well as defending Calais and the English south coast. They might well prevent a full-scale French invasion if such were tried. And why should the French not attempt that? They had mounted one in the eleventh century which had been completely successful at little cost.

The king knew that southern nations relied on rowed galleys - easily manoeuvred and ideal for action in the Mediterranean - but he realised that for rougher northern waters only sails were practical. It was no secret that French naval armament was superior to the English, so Henry set out to obtain at least parity as soon as possible. For this end, the magnificent natural harbour of Portsmouth was supplied with a dry dock. The nearby extensive New Forest, with inexhaustible supplies of hard timber, was to provide the building material.

Enormous numbers of men were employed in this great undertaking. The tall oaks of the royal hunting forest were felled and brought out over rough tracks to the shipyard at Portsmouth. Italian shipwrights were employed to begin with and expected to teach their skills to English tradesmen.

Two keels were laid in 1509 and it was estimated that the complete task would take two years. The ships' fire power was to be a copy of the heavy land-based armament. Everything was decorated in Tudor times, and warships were no exception, with wood carvings and elaborate designs cast on the guns. Accommodation was planned for numbers of billmen and pikemen as well as archers and sailors. The captains chosen to command the warships already had experience of naval warfare, but the men were mostly raw recruits.

Chapter Two

Incredible as it sounds, widower Henry, not long after the death of his wife, was making soundings in foreign courts for a second partner. The reader has probably guessed that the principal requirement of the successful candidate was a very healthy dowry. Wealth had become for him the over-riding consideration of his life.

About two years before Queen Elizabeth died, the king was putting out feelers in Europe for offers for the hand of the Princess Mary who was then an infant of five. Her great beauty, already being commented upon beyond the shores of England, was an asset, and if the husband selected were rich, then only a small dowry would be demanded. The most favoured prince was Charles of Austria and Castile, who was slightly younger than Mary, and the grandson of the Emperor Maximilian on one side and Ferdinand and Isabella of Spain on the other. His parents were Philip the Fair of Austria and Joan of Castile, so the little boy had a title from each parent. King Henry was enthusiastic but the Austrian Philip less so, although he pretended agreement. It was said that secretly he wanted a Spanish bride for his Charles.

Negotiations were continuing in a half-hearted way which suited Philip when he and his wife Joan were shipwrecked on the Dorset coast in 1506. Henry at once wanted to profit by the happy accident, and invited the stranded couple to be entertained at Windsor before taking another ship to Spain. Joan was not well after her ordeal, but Philip set out alone and was met along the road by the young Prince Henry (Duke of York) who escorted him to the castle where he was joined a week later by Joan who had by now fully recovered physically but not mentally as emerged later.

It was a heaven-sent opportunity. The usual merry-making

began, centering round food and drink, with half the night spent at table. But there was also dancing, jokes and tricks by jesters, singing and acrobats. Mary was overjoyed and determined to join in everything. Katherine also was more than happy to see unexpectedly her Spanish relations. Now that Mary was motherless, she always appeared in public with Katherine on the king's orders. Although only nine, Mary received Joan, Reigning Queen of Castile, with great self-assurance and every attention to the details of court etiquette.

The Princess was pleased to be the centre of a royal show for the first time and the king was delighted to watch her success. The royal guests were in raptures over her looks and accomplishments. She danced solos gracefully and professionally before the whole court, and talked charmingly in French, demonstrating an unexpected fluency. She frequently played the gentle lute, solo and as an accompaniment to her sweet small voice. It was said that some of her audience were in tears when she sang the sad plaintive songs of unrequited and hopeless love then so popular. Not shy, not pert, she waited until invited to perform. Then smiling her sweet smile of acceptance and dropping a curtsey to the royals, she called for her lute. Settling herself in her special small chair in the centre of the floor, she carefully tuned her diminutive instrument and began to charm the distinguished assemblage.

After several weeks of this at Windsor, King Henry escorted his guests to London - the poor little charity boys of Eton with their monk-teachers turned out to cheer as the royal cavalcade trotted by - and bade them farewell as they boarded a ship for Spain.

During the visit Henry, in addition to trying to finalise Mary's marriage proposals, suggested himself as a suitable bridegroom for Philip's sister Duchess Margaret of Savoy, and his son, Henry of York, as a husband for Eleanora of Austria. None of these weddings took place. Philip of Austria looked ill all the time he was in England, and indeed he died the next year. Even less fortunate was Queen Joan, who became demented and never recovered her reason Henry was not seemingly deterred by insanity, for a rich dowry prompted him to ask to marry that poor soul. "Madness does not mean she is infertile," he wrote.

The matter of Mary's marriage settlement dragged on endlessly with the Princess becoming increasingly impatient at the delay. During the long wait, the children had exchanged many formal, but very touching, letters expressing their mutual affection. Eventually and at long last, in 1508 at Richmond

Palace, Mary was married to Charles by proxy - the Sieur de Bergues from Flanders undertaking the office of bridegroom. The usual protracted royal entertainments took place, the Princess Katherine of Wales being chaperone to the bride. Mary, now called Princess Mary of Castile, received great diamonds and pearls from Charles as a wedding present and from his grandfather, Emperor Maximilian, an enormous ruby enclosed with a pearl surround. More rubies came from Charles' aunt Margaret, Dowager Duchess of Savoy.

Mary of Castile made a formal speech of thanks and acceptance which she had learned by heart. Instead of kissing her hand or embracing her, De Bergues, as proxy husband, now kissed her on the lips. Bishops and other notables signed as witnesses to the contract and a High Mass was celebrated before the court attended the wedding breakfast. All the dishes and plates on the tables were of gold, as were the elaborate épergnes and salt cellars.

Henry VII paid to the wedding delegation an amount of fifty thousand crowns dowry money, and in exchange, a cluster of enormous diamonds was deposited in England as a guarantee that the money would be repaid if the marriage failed to take place. Evidently the king had not much confidence in the word of Maximilian.

Mary, Katherine and their ladies were able to watch the joustings from a balcony in their apartments which overlooked the tilt-yard at Richmond.

After this event, the king began to lose interest in happenings outside the palace and courtiers noticed that his strength was gradually failing. They spoke of his "grave infirmity". Realising that life was ebbing, Henry examined his conscience and began to make some atonement for the forced loans made during his reign. As an earnest of this, he commanded the release from London prisons of those whose conviction was relative to debts of less than two pounds. After asking pardon of all those he had wronged, he died a peaceful death in April 1509. All his life he loved great ceremony and his magnificent funeral was an acknowledgment of this. The Requiem Mass was attended by his son Henry (who succeeded as Henry VIII) and by his daughter Princess Mary of Castile together with the Dowager Princess of Wales. Benedictine monks of Westminster Abbey sang the mass and the burial took place in the Henry VII chapel where, as he asked, his corpse was laid beside that of his wife Elizabeth. His effigy carried in the procession was made from the actual death mask.

Mary's father, the first Tudor king, was known both in

England and abroad as a miser who ruined many of his subjects by taxation in the form of forced loans and "gifts". Less well known was his encouragement of trade and exploration in the New World across the Atlantic, now just beginning. He was patron and sponsor of the Cabot expedition from Bristol when Newfoundland in Canada was discovered. He also fostered the translation and printing of foreign books.

His manner was always solemn and dour but after his queen's death he became morose and difficult with his family and court. It was said he just did not know how to smile. It was known among his intimates that he had never been unfaithful to his queen. She was aware of this and appreciated the virtue unusual in monarchs of the time.

Mourning for the king was a very short fifteen weeks, but the pleasure-loving young monarch was in a hurry to bid farewell to the gloom of his father's court. He was in a hurry about another matter too, for he lost no time at all in marrying Katherine of Aragon in the summer of 1509. Barely two weeks later, the couple went to the Tower to spend a traditional visit in the fortress before being crowned in Westminster Abbey. The great procession to the abbey was a marked success, with all London in the streets to cheer. Henry himself was a magnificent figure on a huge horse, revelling in his popularity. Mary of Castile, being the only sister of the king, had a prominent part to play in the processions and at the coronation ceremony all of which she enjoyed. As to be expected, she wore many wonderful dresses and took the opportunity of donning the very valuable if rather showy jewelry given by Charles of Austria and his relations.

The coronation banquet itself was exceptionally extravagant, with more than thirty courses of rich food. As laid down by tradition, two Maids of Honour sat under the table for the whole of that gargantuan meal holding the queen's napkin, fan and purse. Other noble ladies stood behind Katherine's chair with cloths in case she wished to spit or wipe her face.

During these festivities the court watched while savage hunting dogs were released into an enclosure with a small herd of deer. Some deer managed to jump the fence and, pursued by the dogs, rushed into the palace corridors where they were soon killed, the carcases being presented to the new queen.

This was to be the happiest time of Katherine's life. She had the love of a wonderful husband and affection of a sister-in-law. Everything was going to be great fun from now on. The arrears of her dowry had arrived from Spain and she now had money to pay her debts and plenty for current expenditure after having been long denied this. She could not believe her good fortune in securing the handsome and virile Henry who could have chosen almost any other princess in Europe. And all this after so many dark years of worry and anxiety. Katherine now began to learn English and soon became fluent in speaking and reading.

As Duke of York, Prince Henry was popular, but as King Henry VIII even more so. He was very handsome, with an instant smile of welcome. Physically extremely strong, he was an open-air type, who loved jousting and wrestling, hunting and tennis. Astoundingly, he was also a musician (his instrument: the lute) and a composer. His voice was strong and accurate. A linguist, he spoke French and Latin approaching perfection, and had a good knowledge of Italian and Spanish. As an accomplished dancer, he learned all the complicated set dances of the period. He had a loud laugh, and enjoyed his jester's jokes, as well as the practical variety. His sense of humour enabled him to laugh at himself. An intellectual, he wrote prose and poetry. An enthusiastic and very pious son of the Church, he wrote a book defending the Faith and was rewarded the title of *defensor fidei* by the Pope. He appreciated good food and good wine, but as he grew older he changed from gourmet to gourmand. Henry VII was lucky in his children, for his namesake son was the perfect young hearty male and Mary the extremely beautiful epitome of femininity.

With a boisterous king aged eighteen, a twenty-two-year-old queen looking forward to some pleasure after years of frustration, a princess just thirteen, it is not surprising that laughter rang through palaces and that there was much romping and horseplay. All three enjoyed dressing up, dancing and rather childish games. Simple pastimes were much in favour: Hide and Seek, Hunt the Slipper, Tag, Charades, Squirting People with Coloured Water. Ladies rode their palfreys up staircases and through palace corridors and were sometimes attacked by courtiers dressed as wild savages or ogres. There was much excitement to be had struggling, screaming and running away from the "captors". All this chasing about was much better for youngsters than sitting for hours at a table as course after course after course was served.

Mary was now very important. She came next to the queen in precedence and was the proxy wife of the heir of the Emperor Maximilian. She revelled in her title of Princess Mary of Castile and in all the deference shown to her.

These many amusements stopped for a time as mourning for Mary's grandmother was decreed for the court. This aged lady, Margaret Beaufort, Countess of Richmond, had been at the centre of all the struggles of the Wars of the Roses. She was a mistress of intrigue and court manoeuvres, yet managed to keep her head on her shoulders: no mean feat in those times. The countess loved her granddaughter and remembered her in her will. One of the bequeathed items was a large gold cup much bejewelled.

On January 1st 1511, to the king's great joy, Katherine gave birth to a son, christened Henry by the Archbishop of Canterbury. Although lively at birth, the little prince began ailing after two weeks and the queen noticed that he was not as strong as at first thought. The king, being told of this, went at once on a pilgrimage to the Norfolk shrine of Our Lady of Walsingham as a thanksgiving for the birth combined with a petition that the boy would grow to manhood. There were fantastic celebrations at court for the birth of little Henry. Bonfires blazed and banquet succeeded banquet.

King Henry was well able to play the spendthrift at the beginning of his reign, for his father had left a full treasury. As soon as the coronation was over, he plunged without delay into matrimonial politics - a great occupation for European courts in the sixteenth century. Marriages were frequently made between infants and even babies in their cradles, but as there was ample time between engagement or proxy marriage and puberty, most of these "marriages" were not consummated. In fact, princelings were frequently married several times in their minority with arrangements subsequently cancelled according to whether treaties of friendship were retained in force or repudiated. Enemies became friends and friends became enemies, often at the personal whim of a monarch.

In the sixteenth century, it became a court custom to allow the public to watch royalty dining - mostly at a state banquet. The spectators were confined behind a rope or barrier. These people were generally higher grade civil servants, minor nobility or foreigners (frequently merchants) resident in the capital. In other words they came from backgrounds generally associated with good behaviour. This did not always prevent a running commentary being made and occasionally reaching royal ears.

When outdoor parties were held - dancing in fancy dress, fireworks, bonfires, acrobatic displays - a mob of common folk was allowed in to watch, but always behind strong barriers. This kind of public came to see their betters have their fun, but as a bonus from time to time, food in the form of plate leavings was distributed. Londoners were known to be cheeky and not easy to control, so on these open air occasions opportunities were obvious.

One of these parties was held in honour of the newly born prince-heir. The mise-en-scene was particularly luxurious. It happened that some golden ornaments used in the pageant carelessly dangled too close to the fence, and some of the mob began to stretch out their hands to snatch them. In this they were successful, and immediately things got out of hand - everyone wanted his piece of gold. In no time at all the barriers were overturned and there was a huge break-in of the crowd.

The scenery was soon bare of its golden ornaments and then the rioters turned their attention to the courtiers from whom were snatched earrings, necklaces, rings, while gentlemen of the court, attendants and guards struggled to control the rabble. The Lord Steward made unsuccessful efforts to stop the pillage quickly, for ladies and gentlemen were being roughly stripped of their clothes. The queen herself was being assaulted by thieves, and court ladies screamed in terror. King Henry had already lost his doublet and drawers and would soon be quite naked, as many of the courtiers already were, before the guards restored order by beating the mob with heavy sticks. When the riot was over, the king roared with laughter and asked everyone to treat the whole incident as a joke, which the courtiers were obliged to do, although greatly upset and distressed. He ordered that nobody was to be punished over the incident.

Henry then took the queen's hand and led her into the palace with the court following. All were somewhat dirty and even bruised, with clothing either torn or somewhat missing, but everyone now treated it as a great piece of fun. There was much laughter at table that evening and it was talked about with amusement long afterwards. Sadly, the little boy in whose honour this party was held died after less than two months on earth. His parents were greatly distressed but Henry did all he could to assist his wife to get over her disappointment and recover her spirits. The entry in the state records reads:

> In the second year of Our Lord the King's reign Her Grace the Queen bore a prince whose soul is now among the Holy Innocents of God.

England's new king was one to enjoy life to the full, and by this he meant the pleasures of the table, the bed and the hunt.

But he was also an intellectual and a politician. He was always kept up to date with news from European courts and inherited a love/hate relationship with France, which had existed for many centuries. The two countries bickered all the time they were at peace, but when at war, they both longed for peace, apparently seeing how futile it was to quarrel, being such near neighbours. But whether at peace or at war, unofficial raids on coastal villages in the Channel seemed to continue, for the loot always came in useful.

Why these wars occurred intermittently nobody had discovered, for the two countries had much in common. French was the court language of both, and was spoken fluently by the nobility. Scholars had a common language in Latin. Both nations were Catholic. French fashions were copied in England. English students crowded French universities. Frenchmen were often bishops of English sees. English travellers to Italy and Spain were a common sight on French roads. There was no territorial dispute, for by now only the tiny Calais enclave belonged to England, while France no longer claimed the Channel Islands.

In spite of all this, Henry VII had been frightened of his neighbour and had initiated his large naval programme. His huge warship, the *SOVEREIGN*, whose re-building was well under way on the stocks could not be far from a completion date.

At that period, the army and the navy were the personal charge of the monarch. Although Henry VII was mean, he had not flinched at spending on the armed forces. Henry VIII was busily spending the treasure amassed by his father, but he too thought it necessary to strengthen the navy - a decision in this case probably purely a matter of international prestige - and he gave the order for the keels of two more great ships to be laid at Portsmouth. To make that dockyard and port safe from raiders, Henry also decided to build a series of low castles along the shore line of Spithead and the Solent. These were designed to have great fire-power against enemy warships and also to prevent troop landings on the beaches and flat cliffless coast.

Several thousand extra workers were recruited for timber felling and ship construction, so Portsmouth town grew and was prosperous. Eventually, in 1511, the ships took to the water, and a grand sight they were, riding in the sheltered harbour. The larger, destined to be the flagship, was named *MARY ROSE* in honour of the king's sister the Princess Mary Tudor: Mary for her Christian name and Rose for the emblem of the House of Tudor - a double rose of alternate red and white petals. The princess must have been thrilled with the compliment, although there is no mention of it in her extant correspondence. This is not surprising, as she was resident at court, seeing her brother and other relatives almost daily.

The other ship was named by Henry in honour of the Queen *PETER POMEGRANATE* that fruit being the emblem of Katherine's native country: Andalucia. So there was no jealousy - both the women nearest and dearest to the king had been equally honoured. Both ships had four masts and carried a great area of sail. Both were luxurious vesels equipped for entertaining distinguished visitors. This was important, as royalty often used warships for private social and state occasions. When on active service, the *MARY ROSE* carried about five hundred fighting men.

The first voyage of these two new ships was in 1511, from Portsmouth up the Channel to the Thames, to receive final equipment and armament from the armoury at the Tower of London. For this trip, a skeleton crew had been aboard, but now the ships were to be fully manned. Recruiting parties went to Bristol and Norfolk and marched the men back to London where their ships were waiting in the river.

The court moved constantly between various places on the river. Even near London the roads were bad, so royal barges were used and were a common and splendid sight, with their uniformed oarsmen working in rhythm, pennants flying and sometimes musicians entertaining the passengers. Moving between Greenwich, Westminster, the Tower, Baynard's Castle, Richmond Palace, Hampton Court and several other houses in company with Katherine the Queen, Mary must have many times seen her ship namesake. Henry had the habit of entertaining at small dinner parties on board his ships, so perhaps the two women did go on board sometime during the whole year the king's navy was lying idle somewhere between Greenwich and the Tower.

About this time it is thought that the Princess Mary, then in her mid-teens, fell in love with Charles Brandon, Duke of Suffolk. The Princess had known Charles Brandon as a baby in arms. He was the boyhood friend of her brother Arthur and later of brother Henry - particularly of Henry. Brandon was born in about 1481, and so was approximately ten years older than the prince. Brandon's father had been killed by Richard III when, as standard bearer, he was protecting Henry of

27

Richmond (later Henry VII) at the battle of Bosworth Field. When Richmond ascended the throne he wished to show his gratitude for the brave action, and brought up the son at his court.

Although there was a difference in age, Prince Henry of York and the orphan Brandon made firm and excellent friends. They both liked the same things. Both were handsome and of magnificent physique. Of virile aspect, both were wonderful horsemen, both excellent shots. They both enjoyed wrestling and usually unseated opponents in the lists. Both had enormous appetites for food and drink. Even as teenagers they were womanisers. At court both loved dancing and games which involved rough horseplay.

But there were differences. Henry was intelligent, a scholar and a musician. Charles Brandon was a Philistine - he could not spell, and wrote a letter only with difficulty.

Charles had married the daughter of Sir Anthony Browne but then managed to have the marriage annulled on a technicality. Looking carefully around, he then wedded Lady Mortimer, twice his age and a very wealthy widow, which possibly explains the attraction. It was not long before her fortune was spent and it was then discovered that the annulment of his previous marriage was not valid and so Brandon returned to his first wife and by her had two daughters.

It was perhaps inevitable that Mary was attracted to Brandon, for he was constantly at court and without any doubt extremely attractive to women. It seems that, when Brandon first realised what feeling he had aroused, he was in a great panic, but then slowly let her know that it was reciprocated. Mary herself was unknowingly a strong magnet to men, being a great beauty with sweet feminine qualities, including a ready smile. The situation was fraught with grave danger, for friend or no friend, Henry would not hesitate to cut off Brandon's head if it was thought he was aspiring to the hand of a Princess of the Blood Royal. Mary was less worried than he was, for she thought as her brother loved her he would raise no objection to marriage with a commoner. Brandon had to warn her that the king would certainly punish her severely. Their love seemed hopeless. Mary had already married Charles of Castile by proxy and Brandon was a married man with a family.

Brandon shied away from becoming more involved, for he was unwilling to risk a career and even life itself for a young girl just because she was the loveliest in Europe. Nevertheless, some sort of understanding was reached between them. No notes were passed. No glances exchanged in company. There were furtive smiles in palace corridors, warm shy looks, a hand squeeze or a few whispered words. Nothing else. Even so, it was amazing that in the centre of such a busybody court only the merest rumour was heard. Even when the listener discounted the tale, for both Mary and Brandon covered their traces so expertly that the story was not believed. The princess was such an innocent little creature, so obedient to her royal brother's slightest wish, that such conduct as flirting with a mere courtier was unthinkable.

Since the 1508 proxy marriage, Mary's "matter" had dragged on. Sometimes the little bridegroom was slow in answering Mary's letters and, occasionally, the correspondence ceased completely. Every letter finished by looking forward to the day they could be together but no action was taken to hasten it. The stop/go affair was very frustrating to Mary until she understandably wished it could be called off altogether, for she began to despair of ever getting married. She knew, of course, that everything depended on the international situation which seemed always to be in a state of flux. When the Austria/Spain/England alliance was in full swing then detailed plans were made, including plans for the trousseau, but then one of those powers made a treaty (secret or open) with France and Mary was back to square one.

Occasionally, definite rumours came to England that the Emperor had changed his mind and was looking for a Spanish bride for his grandson, but then the Spanish Ambassador, Fuensalida, rushed to court to reassure King Henry telling him that the marriage had not been called off, and that without any doubt it would be consummated in the end. It was found out later that this see-saw attitude on the part of the ambassador was the express order of Maximilian - he always liked to keep a political ace up his sleeve. Right from the beginning, Mary had looked forward to the marriage but no thought at all was given to the young people, who were only pawns in the larger political game.

In 1512, the old see-saw went down the other way with a bump, and England (with allies Austria and Spain) declared war on France. Henry went off with his army to fight from his Calais base with the queen saying goodbye at Dover. Katherine had been appointed regent while the king was in France. From her letters it can be seen that she had made great progress in English, for they are clear and concise. It is apparent from her correspondence that she disliked Cardinal Wolsey, Lord Chancellor of England. She disapproved of his overweening pride, his love of luxury, his ruthless ambition to be Pope and his loose morals (he maintained a regular mistress who travelled with him). Such conduct in clergy made her very angry.

Katherine also recoiled from his lack of manners, which betrayed his butcher-boy origin, but was forced to admire his fantastic brain and outstanding memory, as well as his natural ability to organise. Like Thomas à Becket in an earlier century, Wolsey was trying to do the impossible - work in a high position for church *and* state and was already riding for a fall, given the volatile temperament of the king.

To Mary's great joy, her friendship with the queen had been renewed. A little while since, when depressed that no letters had arrived from Charles of Castile, she had blamed this on Katherine, who she imagined was intriguing with her Spanish relations. Eventually Mary discovered that these suspicions were completely unfounded, and the cloud disappeared. The intimacy of these two friends then continued right until Mary's death. When war with France was declared, Charles wrote again in the warmest terms, and the romance went on as before, with Mary's happy reply being sent immediately.

As soon as war was declared, King Henry mobilised the fleet then lying in the Thames. Its task was primarily to keep the Channel open for its whole length and protect the south coast. Secondly, it was charged with destroying the French fleet so that no invasion could be effected. The court was at Greenwich at the time, and it is very likely that the queen and the Princess would have watched the large fleet sail seaward Their two warships the flagship *MARY ROSE* and the *PETER POMEGRANATE* were going into action for the first time. It was usual for the court to cluster at the palace windows to watch warships sail past, and it surely happened on that occasion when the whole of the fleet departed. The big ships presented a grand sight with their huge sails and enormously long pennants streaming out in the breeze. Orders shouted to the sailors could always be heard clearly across the narrow water.

The ships successfully swept the Channel without encountering much opposition, and then returned to Portsmouth. Henry was delighted with his navy and went down himself to congratulate his admiral Sir Edward Howard. A large banquet on board the flagship *MARY ROSE* was given by the king to his senior officers, some local dignitaries and the gentlemen in attendance. Warships were always well equipped for first-class entertaining, which meant ten to twenty courses and barrels of Spanish or Portuguese wine.

It was not long before the fun and games had to be abruptly stopped, for English spies reported that the French fleet was massing in Breton ports. At once, the English navy left Portsmouth to carry out their second aim of the destruction of their French opponents. On arrival off the coast of Brittany, the English admiral attacked with full fire-power, taking the French completely by surprise, for their senior officers were busily entertaining local grandees. This gave the English an immediate advantage.

The *MARY ROSE* chose the French flagship *GRANDE LOUISE*, and a fierce engagement ensued. Over three hundred soldiers and sailors died on the French ship, and as the admiral thought her in danger of sinking, he ordered her to retire from the battle to avoid being taken as a prize. The crew of the *MARY ROSE* were disappointed to see the *GRANDE LOUISE* disengage and seek shelter, as it meant for them the loss of their prize money, which would have amounted to a small fortune for each.

The action continued just as savagely, with great damage being done by the broadsides from the *MARY ROSE*. It was obvious that many thousands of Frenchmen and a smaller number of English had been killed or drowned, but for several more days the flagship cruised off the coast looking for a fight before the enemy retreated to Brest. The admiral reported that his ship had accounted for thirty-two ships - sunk or taken as prizes - casualties caused by arms or drowning now quite uncountable. As well as this, there were many French prisoners held below decks. It was a fine hour for *MARY ROSE* and a tremendous victory for England. The fame of the flagship was fully deserved for she had done by far most of the work.

Did the princess hear of the success of her namesake? Most assuredly she did, for little else was talked about at court and in the country at large. A victory over the French was always popular, for France had not yet been supplanted by Spain as the permanent enemy. And when the news reached Mary she could have felt no other feeling than pride.

The year 1513 was an exciting year for the Princess Mary

of Castile, for Charles Brandon and for England. Brandon's wife, Anne Browne, died leaving him two daughters. Losing no time, Charles became engaged to the heiress of the wealthy Lord Lisle and somehow obtained from the king the title of Baron Lisle: a somewhat premature action for he had not yet married the lady. He accompanied his king to fight in France, where Henry was victorious in the Battle of the Spurs, seizing the towns of Therouanne and Tournai. On his way back to Calais and home, Henry met at Lille the young Archduke Charles of Austria, Prince of Castile and proxy husband of Mary. With him was his aunt the Archduchess Margaret of Austria, Dowager Duchess of Savoy, who was Regent of the Spanish Netherlands. The English king at once liked the young Charles and thought him intelligent and very suited as a brother-in-law.

It would seem that the archduchess was in a rather frivolous mood and apparently, having watched and admired the handsome and dashing Brandon in action at jousting, gave Charles the notion that she was swept off her feet. King Henry, possibly in jest, promoted a love-making scene between the two, acting as interpreter. Charles Brandon was quite used to making easy conquests of the fair sex, and played along with the conversation. Eventually, he gave the impression that he was paying serious court to the royal lady. To make matters worse, Henry was now making deliberately false translations and then, carrying the joke still further, made Margaret repeat obscene English words, not knowing their meaning. All three laughed heartily until the archduchess suspected all was not quite as she had thought, and abruptly put Brandon in his place: "He is not a mate for me." She reminded him sharply of the gap between her rank and his - a gap unbridgeable. His lordship retreated much sobered by the snub.

Before Henry returned to England with many noble hostages - including the royal Duc de Longueville - it was arranged that the following year, the matter of Mary's marriage would be finalised at Calais, as all dowry difficulties would by then have been resolved. While King Henry was abroad, under the regency of Queen Katherine the English army had inflicted a disastrous defeat on the Scots at Flodden Field. In thanksgiving for this victory, Katherine made an official pilgrimage to her favourite shrine of Our Lady at Walsingham. The king of Scotland, James IV, was killed at this Battle of Flodden and Katherine had his body embalmed and kept unburied until Henry had made his wishes known. On his return to England, it was decided that, as James had died while excommunicated, it was better kept in store in a room at the monastery of Shene. Much later on, the corpse could not be found and it was thought that the Scottish king had not been given decent burial, as according to the law of the church it should have been.

The naval war continued with short skirmishes which decided nothing - it was a kind of cold war. Rather imprudently, the king ordered his fleet to leave the Channel and take part in a royal review to be held in the Thames off Greenwich. The palace there was a favourite one of successive kings. It was an enormous pile - a real rabbit warren. Full of staircases, corridors, bricked-up doors, very small useless rooms, it had been added to haphazardly over the centuries and, it was rumoured, contained many residents who had no right to be there in the first place. It was inconvenient and almost falling to pieces, but royalty liked it because it was cosy and intimate and beautifully situated on the river. The palace was surrounded by a magnificent park with good hunting. Royal barges were kept on the river for easy transport to other palaces, for barges were extemely fast, slim boats with a large number of oarsmen of skill and strength. The passengers were under shelter in bad weather, and the ride was comfortable, unlike the jolting journeys by coach over tracks which passed for roads. At a naval review, the ships passed before King, Royal Family and court standing at riverside windows. At that time "Royal Family" meant Queen Katherine and the Princess Mary of Castile.

King Henry loved his fleet and was proud of it. He enjoyed going abroad. On this occasion, his family with some ambassadors and courtiers visited several ships and there was some very extravagant entertaining.

This review convinced His Grace that his navy was still not big enough, and accordingly he ordered another keel to be laid. That ship became the *IMPERIAL* and shortly afterwards yet another keel went down. This latest ship was the super warship named *HENRI GRACE A DIEU* which later became known affectionately as the *GREAT HARRY*.

The *MARY ROSE* and her attendant fleet had still not succeeded in completely destroying the French navy, in spite of the recent resounding victory. The king wanted annihilation, nothing less. And so he ordered his ships once again to the Brittany coast, but this time with the added task of burning

33

Brest - naval port and town. As before, Admiral Sir Edward Howard was in command and his flagship was still the *MARY ROSE*.

The English lost no time in establishing a blockade and landed a large contingent to carry out the burning, but the task was found more difficult than the admiral thought. In view of later discipline problems, it may have been that the men were more interested in looting than in burning. While this operation was in progress, some French war galleys appeared, coming from the Mediterranean under the command of Admiral de Bidoux. He at once made tremendous efforts to break the blockade but was not able to do so.

The two navies were now engaged in a great battle, during which the English admiral, Sir Edward Howard, was pushed overboard and drowned. Strangely, the next senior officer failed to take command, and now without a leader or firm orders, the fleet abandoned the action and sailed for England. This disgraceful incident was probably caused by lack of training of the second-in-command, which really meant that the possibility of the admiral becoming a casualty had not been adequately arranged for. The king then appointed as admiral on board the *MARY ROSE* Sir Thomas Howard (later Earl of Surrey), who was elder brother to Sir Edward. The new admiral took command at Dartmouth in May 1513.

Apparently Sir Thomas was a strict disciplinarian and perhaps for that reason had been chosen, for order had sadly broken down in the fleet in general and on the *MARY ROSE* in particular. Known as a very hard man, the admiral maintained this discipline until the war with France had ended.

Obedience just had to be enforced on board ship in those days for a mutiny could easily flair up. Crews were for the most part pressed into service, and many were from the city with no connection at all with the sea. Men were cramped for space in the dark, below-deck quarters, eating poor and sometimes rotten food, bothered by vermin and poorly clad. Fire was a real fear on a wooden ship lit by candles. A mere spark from an arsonist could destroy a magnificent ship with a great deal of explosive aboard. Much submissive muscle power was essential with great sails and heavy ropes, so men given to slowness in obeying an order suffered savage punishments: floggings, irons - even throwing overboard in serious cases of incitement to mutiny. One thing united officers and men - the hope of taking of loot from enemy ships. A good catch could make all the difference to the entire crew.

While the *MARY ROSE* was in Devon, the French took

advantage and landed by night at the large village of Brighton, burnt it to the ground after looting and then retreated when some English archers appeared over the Downs. During the rearguard action, the French admiral was wounded in the face and lost an eye. Shortly afterwards, the English retaliated, burning and plundering several French villages on the Normandy and Picardy coasts.

Throughout the up-and-down, on-and-off engagement of Mary to Prince Charles of Castile, the Spanish Ambassador Fuensalida was always at Henry's elbow keeping him convinced that King Ferdinand and the Emperor Maximilian wanted very much, as Charles himself, the marriage to be consummated with the young couple living happily together. When political relations with Spain were good, then His Excellency the Ambassador found small reasons for a postponement, at least for a time. When political relations were bad, then Fuensalida emphasized that the hitch was only a temporary one. All this subtle diplomacy was carried out on the direct orders of Ferdinand of Spain.

Sometimes the ambassador brought affectionate notes from Charles to Mary, praising her beauty and telling her he could not wait for the moment when they became really man and wife. These notes signed "Votre Bon Mari" sent Mary into raptures, promising the prince her complete submission and life-long devotion.

What finally upset the apple cart was King Henry's discovery that behind his back Ferdinand had signed a truce with the French King Louis. It is not known whether Henry was playing a double game to frustrate the Spanish double game, or whether he was really deceived by Fuensalida's subtlety. But whether the English king's patience gave out, or whether scales dropped from his eyes, an announcement was made that the proxy marriage had finally ended. The ambassador quickly asked for an audience and tried to persuade Henry that it was cruel to separate a young couple who loved each other so intensely, at the same time vaguely offering some concession in the matter of number and value of dowry diamonds. But it was all too late. The king finally had had enough.

Neither Charles nor Mary were consulted in any way. They were merely informed that their contract was at an end. The reaction of the prince is not known, but Mary was greatly distressed. There was much weeping, even hysteria, and a very angry scene with her brother, but to no avail. So deep-rooted was the tradition that royalty was obliged to make political marriages that the court thought Mary was being most unreasonable.

Chapter Three

After the Battle of the Spurs in 1513, the most important prisoner taken by the English was a prince of the Blood Royal of France, Louis d'Orleans, Duc de Longueville. The amount of ransom money paid by the families of prisoners (often kept as hostages) depended on rank. A royal prisoner was therefore very valuable.

The Duke was treated as royalty by Henry and sent to Katherine under escort. She was asked to entertain the prisoner hospitably. Understandably, the queen was displeased by this suggestion and it was indeed incredible that Henry should have made such a request. Just how a Queen of England could be hostess and jailer at the same time was not clear. Always the diplomat, Katherine explained that her palace was unable to provide efficient security and added that it was her intention in any case to travel north to take charge of the country's defence against a Scottish attack. Scotland, as always, was taking advantage of England's involvement on the continent to make trouble along the border, with the help of English dissidents.

Queen Katherine consulted Wolsey and made the sensible proposal that the French duke be sent to the Tower, the most secure prison in England. Later, de Longueville was released, and when hostilities with France ceased, he became an honoured guest at Henry's court.

After making her thanksgiving pilgrimage to Walsingham for Scotland's defeat, the queen took up residence at Richmond Palace where she was joined by the victorious king, who expressed his pleasure at her management of the country as regent. He did not tell her, but he brought with him from France an exceptionally beautiful mistress, the married Lady Tailbois, whom he installed secretly in an Essex Manor House which he called his "Pleasure House". Later he had a son by this mistress whom he created Duke of Richmond.

Although the queen did her best to comfort her, Mary lived in a state of extreme agitation which can easily be understood. After all these years of shilly-shallying, at the age of eighteen, after a long engagement, she found herself pushed back again on the marriage market. For years she had carried the title of Princess Mary of Castile proudly as a married woman. She felt repudiated and horribly ashamed and hurt. It was an ordeal now to face court ceremonies. It was doubly hurtful because she could only blame her brother of whom she was genuinely fond. He had told her of the cancellation of her proxy marriage in a brutal off-hand way, as though the matter was only of slight political importance.

It was true that the highly secret flirting with Brandon continued, but she knew with certainty that he would not risk his head by making this public. She knew that in any case the king would never allow her union with non-royal blood. In spite of the danger, she resolved to try to approach Henry when he was in a good mood and so constantly observed him to seize an opportunity. The king at this time chose to show his regard for his favourite by elevating him to a dukedom and so created him Duke of Suffolk. But now the unfortunate sister was to receive another painful shock - a quite unexpected bombshell.

Out of the blue, the Duc de Longueville suggested to the king that his most beautiful sister become the bride of King Louis XII of France. The Duke made it sound a casual remark, but Louis had ordered him to make a serious enquiry. Instead of the expected rebuff, Henry said he would consider the matter. The more he thought it over, the more he became attracted to the idea. The dowry would be reasonable, he could retain some of the marriage settlement made in cash and jewels and already paid over by the Emperor Maximilian. The French King could not possibly live much longer, and his young widow would come on the marriage market yet again. Then a second political marriage could be negotiated with the costly marriage settlement that a Dowager Queen of France could rightly expect. Yes, the possibilities were very attractive. De Longueville must be told that he looked favourably on the proposal. Henry took it for granted that there would be no opposition from his sister, although he guessed that the English would view with disfavour giving their lovely young princess to an old man.

Mary was called in audience and for a moment just could not believe what was happening. Quite unexpectedly, she at once showed fierce opposition. When she learned of the king's intention she ran to him, screamed incoherently, became quite hysteric, threatened various kinds of destruction of herself, wept, threw herself on the floor before her brother and clung to his knees in spite of his attempts at release. She begged and begged on her knees that his plan should not be proceeded with. Henry was flabbergasted at such disobedience, and then began to point out the advantages of such a union. When this made no impression at all, he told her he would use force - even imprisonment in the Tower. And he meant it. Then he began to coax. Henry told her in detail reports he had received from his ambassador in Paris concerning the king's health, which by now was very precarious. It was thought that at fifty-two years of age he could not possibly last another year. He was thirty-four years older than Mary. Henry did not fail to mention that his sister would be a very wealthy young widow, owning mountains of fabulous jewelry. He admitted that Louis was physically unattractive, but he was known to be very kind and would make a very undemanding and generous husband.

Mary began to wonder whether her brother had heard a whisper about her feeling for the new Duke of Suffolk. She began to realise that her obstinacy was making no progress against the obstinacy of the king. Would she be sacrificed yet again? Could she try to force a compromise, given the chance of an early widowhood? Yes, she would at least try. Better a compromise than facing a lifetime of looking at London from a battlement in the Tower. A wise decision, for she escaped the fate of her descendants and their husbands: Son-in-law Dorset (beheaded), granddaughter Lady Jane Grey and husband Guildford Dudley (beheaded within two days of each other), granddaughters Lady Katherine Grey, Lady Mary Grey, Lady Margaret Clifford (endless years in confinement). Arabella Stuart was sent to the Tower where she became insane. Her husband the Duke of Somerset, who was Mary's great great grandson narrowly escaped severe punishment for marrying her.

She proposed that, if she accepted marriage with Louis, she would receive a firm promise that the second time round she would have an absolutely free choice of her next husband. She did not tell the king whom she had in mind, if anyone at all, but she seemed content with the consent she heard from his own lips. On this condition, she gave her assent to union with the French king. She refused to think that Henry might have given his promise lightly, and perhaps without even thinking, but it must have crossed her mind that his word had been sometimes broken to suit circumstances.

If the year 1514 started badly for Mary, it was a bad year also for the *MARY ROSE*. When peace with France was confirmed, the flagship left the Channel in company with many other ships of the large fleet to lay up in the Thames. Crews were paid off and only a handful of men remained on board *MARY ROSE* to provide a minimum of maintenance, which really amounted to nearly complete neglect - a shameful fate for magnificent ships. The vessels were stripped of sails, fittings and armaments. It was a sad and dismal sight for Londoners during the next ten years. But this was the procedure in those times between sporadic wars.

Greenwich was still a favourite palace of the king (he did not care for Westminster or the Tower). The palace windows gave out on to the river where the naval ships lay deteriorating at anchor or tied up.

When Mary was at Greenwich, she was obliged to see the unwanted ships slowly moving in the current without sign of life. What thoughts could she have had? Perhaps she might have reflected that the *MARY ROSE* had been built to fight France the country which she was now going to enter as queen. Did she still have some affection for the vessel or remember how delighted she was three years before at the compliment paid her by her royal brother?

Without any delay, the Duc de Longueville became busy writing letters and travelling between France and England to arrange for the complicated ceremonies of a proxy marriage in France, a proxy marriage in England and then a final marriage in France with bride and bridegroom present, a coronation at St Denis and great festivities in Paris to mark the arrival of the English queen. In view of the bridegroom's frail health it was necessary to act quickly.

King Louis XII was born in 1462, the son of Charles, Duke of Orléans, and his wife Mary of Cleves. Fatherless at three years old, he had a terrible childhood looked after by unkind attendants. His life and liberty were frequently at risk, as was often the case with any person, even children, within reaching distance of a throne. At an early age he was cruelly forced by King Louis XI to marry his daughter, Princess Jeanne. A truly sad and handicapped creature, it was thought that being deformed and very backward she was unable to conceive and indeed should never have been married at all.

40

Louis hardly ever visited her, ugly and hunchback as she was, although pathetically, she was desperately in love with him.

This strange couple were "married" for over twenty years. Louis XI died in 1483, and Jeanne's teenage brother became King of France. Charles VIII was nearly as deformed as his sister, and of dull intellect. Louis now tried to seize power as regent for King Charles, but the plan failed and the plotter found himself in prison where he stayed for three years. Eventually, Charles died and at long last (aged thirty-six), Louis ascended the French throne, his health ruined by his sufferings.

Pope Alexander VI declared an annulment of the marriage of Louis and Jeanne on the grounds of non-consummation. The unfortunate woman entered a convent to die after six years. Apparently there she found the peace which had for so long been denied her at court.

Louis now hurriedly married Anne of Brittany who was the widow of Charles VIII by whom she had had four children, who all died in infancy. Queen Anne was also deformed in body: one leg was much shorter than the other. But this time, Louis had a happy marriage - he admired his queen and Anne truly loved him. They had two daughters and two stillborn sons, which was a great disappointment to both. However, the province of Brittany was retained by France, which was the object of the marriage.

Early in his reign, Louis decided to invade Italy, conquering the Duchy of Milan, claiming the territory as his by reason of his descent from Duke Gian Galzazzo. The king fought a war in Italy for nearly thirteen years using Milan as a base for operations. Eventually, the French were attacked by the Holy See, Spain and Venice, but they continued the struggle, even though the war was very unpopular in France. In 1513, Louis was finally defeated by the Swiss at Novara, and he was obliged to withdraw across the Alps. At the same time he suffered another defeat by Henry VIII of England at the Battle of the Spurs.

Sensibly, Louis made peace with all his enemies and for the rest of his life there was tranquility in France. His queen, Anne of Brittany, died in 1514, and was buried at St Denis.

His daughter Claude, married François, duc de Valois, Comte d'Angoulême, who now became heir to the French throne: Claude could not succeed Louis as the Salic law in France prohibited a female monarch.

In very indifferent health, King Louis was a sad and lonely man when a widower. Unhappily, he had taken a great dislike to his heir Francis. So when the name of the beauteous Princess Mary was first whispered in his ear he became immediately attracted.

It is not known from what disease Louis was suffering, but it was apparent to the court that he was deteriorating. He had difficulty in walking and in breathing. He had a vacant expression, his lower lip sagged dreadfully and he constantly dribbled. The contrast in the looks of the intended couple was startling - quite like beauty and the beast - for Mary was without rival among the princesses of Europe. Good teeth and good hair were greatly esteemed, and she had both these assets. Fine golden hair fell below her waist when loosened from clasps and nets. Small wonder that poor Louis, now in his dotage, looked forward with excitement to the arrival of his new queen, even if this was mixed with some apprehension.

Louis wanted the wedding as early as possible and so did King Henry, who wanted to avoid a disaster like the previous interminable engagement. Because of Louis' state of health, the negotiations did not last long, and the French king was determined to be very generous. It was arranged that the proxy in France for Mary should be the Earl of Worcester, and the proxy in England for Louis, the Duke of Longueville.

The English ceremony took place on 15th August 1514 at the Grey Friars' Church near Greenwich Palace. Mary was luxuriously dressed; her gown was of shimmering gold with sparkling jewels. She wore a gift from Louis - one of the most famous stones in the world, the "Mirror of Naples" an enormous diamond. Mary spoke her vows clearly and the French duke spoke those on behalf of the husband. There was then a symbolic consummation of the marriage by the Duke and Mary in the presence of the ambassadors and the court. Afterwards the feasting began - ladies and gentlemen were served in separate rooms - followed by lively dancing. The heat was so great that gentlemen of the household were permitted by the king to remove their heavily padded doublets.

The following morning, the Duc de Longueville left for France to make final arrangements for the various ceremonies there. He was the bearer of a letter to Louis:

Monseigneur. I commend myself most humbly to Your Grace. I have received by Monsieur, the Bishop of Lincoln, the very affectionate letters you have written me with your own hand and they have given me infinite joy and comfort. Assure yourself, Monseigneur, that nothing equals my desire to see you and the king, my brother, uses great diligence to speed my passage across the sea which, I hope, by the pleasure of God, will be brief. Meanwhile, I beg that you will afford me the inestimable consolation of often hearing news of your health and happiness. May the aid of our Creator, Monseigneur, grant you a long and prosperous life. From the hand of your very humble consort, Marie.[2]

The French proxy marriage had been celebrated in France on 2nd September in Paris, since when Louis wrote continuously to urge Henry to send him his wife. It was as though Louis feared that the sands of his life would run out before he set eyes on the blond loveliness who had done him the honour of giving her hand. Henry wanted nothing better than a speedy conclusion, and he arranged that he and the queen would travel to Dover to bid formal farewell to the new French consort. Mary's imposing suite took time to assemble and for the necessary transport to be arranged. It totalled over four hundred lords, barons and knights, together with two hundred gentlemen and eighty ladies. Among the ladies was Maid of Honour Anne Boleyn, sister of Mary Boleyn, a former mistress of the king who, after being discarded, had been married off to an obliging courtier. Anne had been included in the royal retinue as she was bilingual, as indeed was Mary herself.

It needed efficient organisation to transport and feed such a large number of persons and their horses - especially such important people with their luxurious wardrobes and their servants. When Mary arrived in Dover and looked down from the castle ramparts she saw quite a large fleet in the roads: many were transports for the suite but others were for the horses and their grooms, and there were also nine escort ships.

When Mary was ready to leave the castle for the beach, a tremendous storm blew up and made embarkation impossible. It was an outsize tempest, which lasted for a whole month, and did great damage throughout the south of England. This made the impatient king very irritable, for he could not leave Dover before his sister had embarked and the castle was uncomfortably crowded, there being nowhere else locally where people could be accommodated. Not only were many of the English suite lodging and eating in the castle, but also quite a large number of a French suite which Louis had previously sent over to Dover to do homage to their new queen.

Eventually this exceptional storm abated, and King Henry profited by the lessening wind to urge the embarkation. The royal party went to the beach where Mary wept, clinging to her

43

brother and sister-in-law embracing them both warmly. The king cut short this lingering farewell, for he was still angry at having decided to go to Dover and at having been shut up stormbound in that overcrowded draughty castle. From the rowing boat, Mary saw the king and queen mount hastily and gallop off to the comfort of Greenwich.

As soon as Mary had gone aboard her cross-channel transport, the fleet sailed. Immediately under way, a second frightening storm broke causing tremendous seas. Progress was virtually impossible and the short crossing took four days and nights. Poor Queen Mary was prostrate with seasickness the whole of that time, and her ladies were unable to be of comfort for all were in a like state. During all the terrible voyage, Mary's ship was alone, for early on, the fleet had become scattered. On the fifth day, the vessel fetched up on a sandbank off Boulogne with great waves breaking over her decks. The captain decided that the royal passenger should be taken to the shore without delay, in case the craft started to break up. On being told of the plan the queen hardly answered, she was so ill. It was her first sea trip ever, and she proved to be a bad sailor. Only those who have experienced prolonged mal-de-mer can appreciate how Mary felt after such an ordeal.

A small rowing-boat came alongside. Mary felt herself lifted in strong arms from her bed, taken on deck and then transferred to other waiting arms - those of Sir Christopher Gervase. On approaching the beach, it was thought that the surf was so heavy the rowing boat might well be overturned, so Sir Christopher (fortunately very tall and very strong) jumped into the sea, lifted Mary out of the boat and strode with her through the breakers. Walking up the sandy beach, he laid Mary Tudor, by now more dead than alive, on land of which she was now queen. Understandably, Mary, cold and soaked to the skin, weak from days of seasickness, was found to be unconscious, but like all sufferers from this malady of the sea, she revived quickly when on firm ground.

When Mary returned to life, she found the Duc de Vendôme kneeling beside her: he had been sent by Louis to welcome her to her new kingdom. Forlorn, bedraggled and wet, there was little of the queen about her at that moment. The Duke soon had her under shelter in a coach, and took her the few kilometres to Boulogne where she was able to rest and recover from her hazardous journey. Louis was waiting for her at nearby Abbeville and was in an agony of fear for her safety, as that town also had experienced great damage from the storm. The king was so delighted when a messenger arrived to say that

Mary was safe in Boulogne that he showed to the Archbishop of Paris and his own immediate entourage an enormous collection of necklaces, rings and bracelets with many unset gems that were destined as presents for his bride. The canny old king told them he would not give all these at one time, but dole them out in dribs and drabs, for he wanted to receive a great number of kisses in return for his treasure. He was so excited that the courtiers felt sure that he would be kind to his new wife and that she would have a good life with him, in spite of his age and invalid condition.

No one was surprised when it was later found that the English fleet which sailed with Mary had suffered much damage. One of the escorting ships, which carried some of the Queen's entourage, had sunk with no survivors.

When fully rested, Mary set out from Boulogne with her retinue to travel by coach and litter the eighty kilometres to Abbeville. The procession went at a gentle pace, and when the weather improved, the ladies mounted palfreys with red velvet saddle-cloths. The numerous suite, all in their most brilliant costumes, made a pretty sight winding over the country roads. After the riders came the closed wagons full of the queen's dresses and the wardrobes of her suite, as well as table plate and cutlery, large tapestries and equipment for a private chapel.

About six kilometres from Abbeville, the procession was met by the Heir Presumptive of France, Duke of Valois, Comte d'Angoulême. Dismounting, he knelt in the dust to kiss the hand of his queen and stepmother. Evidently Francis was impressed by Mary's looks, even though he expected to see beauty. From the pressure of his hand, the queen knew that intimate thoughts were running in the duke's head, and that his feelings were not entirely filial. The Duke announced that the king purposed to ride out from the town to greet his bride on the road.

So the large convoy was stopped to allow the ladies to freshen up in the toilet wagons. These toilet wagons always accompanied travelling royalty especially on long distance journeys. Usually placed at the rear of the procession, they were a combination of bathroom, bucket privy and dressing room - a necessity for comfortable travel. Special attendants were on hand to supply the personal needs of these grand people.

Mary went to the wagon allocated for her own personal use - a wagon much more luxurious than the others. There she changed her clothes ready for meeting her lord and master for the first time. Her costume was a wide farthingale with an elaborate head-dress. And she was really covered with fantastic jewelry. In spite of the gaudiness, her appearance was sweet and virginal, which excited the imagination of all who saw her that day.

The curtains of the horse litter were closed until the great moment when Louis met his queen. The monarch dismounted awkwardly but carefully. Mary made to descend from her litter to kneel before him, but with great thoughtfulness, he noticed the cumbersomeness of her dress and begged her to remain in the litter. The couple embraced. Louis mounted his horse gingerly with the help of attendants, and the docile animal moved sedately on to Abbeville where both king and queen were given a noisy and affectionate welcome.

Louis had been nervous of meeting Mary, but after the wayside meeting he felt he had nothing to fear. He knew he would admire her appearance, but now he was charmed by her manners and grace as well. He was enraptured at the happy smile that told she was pleased with him too. Every inch a queen, she proved she was born royal. She showed no boredom or, what he dreaded most, disgust or repugnance. This made Louis instantly her grateful slave.

As for Mary, she had been very well prepared by her brother for the sad sight of her husband. But Louis was indeed somewhat worse than she imagined for he had no teeth. The constant dribble and the low hanging lip she was prepared for, but the laboured breathing was a shock. Anyone less like a bridegroom could not be conceived. She wondered why he could put himself to so much trouble to re-marry when he must have known that he had not long to live.

She had been told in England by people who knew him that he was very kind and she hoped that this was true. Now she felt sure that it was. At least she was grateful for that, and she firmly made up her mind never to show a feeling of revulsion either to the king himself or to anyone else. She felt she owed him that.

Queen Mary spent three days at Montreuil-sur-Mer en route to Abbeville from Boulogne and stopped again at the village of Etaples to see entertainments by French aristocracy and church dignataries. She saw several elaborate tableaux and scenes, some from the Bible and others on classical themes.

Chapter Four

The ill-matched pair were married in the Cathedral at Abbeville on 9th October 1514, with wonderful traditional ceremonies and magnificent singing. In the morning, Louis presented his bride with a fabulous diamond and ruby necklace which drew all eyes. The queen's dress was a cloth of gold trimmed with royal ermine. She wore a coronet of rubies and sapphires. Throughout the tiring day, she showed no fatigue. She moved gracefully wearing her gentle smile, publicly showing respect and affection for her husband the king. For his part, Louis resolved to show his appreciation in the only way he knew: by showering her constantly with amazing jewels which, in those days as now, were a form of investment.

After the Nuptial Mass, Mary retired to her private apartments with the ladies of the blood royal of France. The gentlemen of the households and ambassadors, with the Duke Francis of Valois, dined in a separate room. Lesser folk feasted in a great hall.

That day, Queen Mary received an exceptional number of jewels. One was a huge diamond cut in a two-pointed way, also two great rubies one five centimetres long and another four. Shortly afterwards, a pile of heavily worked gold chains arrived. The flow of jewelry never seemed to stop.

The following day, the Duke of Norfolk, who had been included in Mary's suite on Henry's orders, had a meeting with her attendants to decide whom she was to keep in France and who was to return to England. But Mary was shocked to discover that Louis had already made the decision himself, and only four Maids of Honour (Anne Boleyn was included) were to remain. Everyone else was to go, even Lady Guildford, who had been the queen's constant companion and governess since babyhood. She was expelled because the wily king

47

sensed she had too much influence over his wife and was far too bossy. He wanted Mary to make her own decisions. Louis also resented Mary speaking a language he did not understand with her household.

Mary dreaded being isolated and wanted around her people she had had for several years in her service and who were familiar with her needs and wishes. She knelt before her new husband begging that his order be rescinded. Overestimating her power with the king, she thought he would give in to her request, but his obstinacy matched hers and she had a point-blank refusal plus another load of jewelry.

Mary did not yet know her lord and tried another tactic. She sat down and wrote:

> My good brother, As heartily as I can commend me to your grace marvelling much that I never heard from you since our departing, so often as I have sent and written to you. Now I am left alone in effect for on the morn next after my marriage my chamberlain, with all other men-servants, were discharged. And in like wise my mother Guildford with other of my women and maidens. If it be by any means possible I humbly require you to cause my mother Guildford to repair hither once again. I am well assured that when ye know the truth of everything as my mother Guildford can show you ye would full little have thought I should be thus entreated. Would to God that my Lord Archbishop of York (Wolsey) had come with me in the room of Norfolk. And thus I beg your grace farewell as ever did prince and wishing you more heartsease than I have now. From Abbeville the 12th October,
> Your Loving Sister,
> Mary, Queen of France.[3]

She wrote a similar letter to Wolsey but Louis was quietly determined to have his way and refused Lady Guildford permission to return to France.

Mary really missed "mother" Guildford and often looked sad and wept or sulked in front of the king, but he did not change his mind. He just ignored her moods and instead produced from the treasury more chains, necklaces and diamond and ruby rings which he himself put on her fingers.

Once back in England, all Mary's dismissed attendants complained loudly to King Henry. Every one of them was disappointed and resentful, for many had accepted a very small wage, hoping that when the princess became the rich Queen of

France they would be generously rewarded. Others, even worse off, had had no wages at all trusting that Mary would make a fine marriage to Charles of Castile and, when that arrangement broke down, an equally profitable union with Louis. Then, they felt sure, their loyalty would be repaid. Instead they were sent back to England peremptorily after being nearly shipwrecked in the Channel, some with clothes ruined, without so much as a thank you. Worse still, they had been obliged to pay their travelling expenses on the return journey. Small wonder that their lamentations were loud.

Louis now suffered the twinges of gout, and demonstrated no enthusiasm for leaving the quiet countryside and hurrying to Paris. He shrank from all the lengthy tiring ceremonies in the capital, all the traditions to be followed. He dreaded the long banquets and court dances, all the endless processions, the robing and de-robing and re-robing, the boring jousts which he had no longer stomach for. But he knew that it had to be faced at some time, and he could not procrastinate indefinitely.

The Earl of Worcester, who was travelling with the royal party, discovered to his amazement that Mary no longer wanted her "mother" Guildford at her side. Every small detail of her life had been so controlled by the governess that she now began to feel the pleasure of being free to make independent decisions. Now as queen all her wishes were gratified and this new freedom she relished.

At the end of October it was judged high time for the coronation to take place, so the huge procession set out on the road once more to stay at Beauvais for a night's rest. From there, it moved through tracks lined with autumn-tinted trees to St Denis, where the royal party had to wait, because the preparations for the coronation were incomplete. That great and touching ceremony could only be held in the magnificent abbey which contained the elaborate tombs of a line of French kings and other royal personages. While waiting at St Denis, the Earl of Worcester asked for an audience, as he had received a letter from King Henry asking if the French king was still opposed to Lady Guildford's return. Louis answered a firm yes, explaining that the governess constantly interfered and sometimes remained in the room even when he wished to be alone with his wife. Mary also confirmed to Worcester that she no longer desired to be served by her former governess. Thankfully then, the whole matter was dropped and no more was heard of the lady's complaints.

Back in England, the king was debating who to send to France as special ambassador to Louis to thank him for his many kindnesses shown to his sister on her arrival and - a dual task - to represent Henry at the queen's coronation. It is thought that the king had a suspicion that before leaving England Mary had a flirtation or a secret understanding with Suffolk and that she had been in love with him. Weighing the matter, he concluded that there was no chance of the romance going further with an anointed queen. In the end, Henry decided to send the duke, who duly arrived at St Denis on his official mission to extend the customary courtesies on the occasion of the queen's crowning.

When the special ambassador arrived at St Denis he was, of course, granted an audience by the king but greatly surprised when he was taken to the royal bedroom to find Louis sitting up in bed with the queen beside him. Suffolk knelt before the king, who motioned him to rise, embraced him warmly with words of welcome and kind enquiries about the health of his dearly loved brother-in-law. The audience was longer than usually allowed, for there was a stream of flowery compliments which enabled the earl to observe the couple. Charles Suffolk reported to England that without doubt Louis and his wife were on excellent terms, appearing to be happy and affectionate. This letter was probably meant to inform Henry indirectly that there was no danger of his ambassador causing a scandal, for the reason that Mary was too much in love with her husband. If that was the intention, then it certainly succeeded, for King Henry's fears were allayed, as so indeed were Wolsey's.

King Louis appointed the sixth of November as the coronation day of the queen. The ceremony of the crowning itself, and the subsequent festivities, required careful organisation, for they were complicated by delicate questions of etiquette and precedence. It was all made somewhat easier, however, because most participants had long experience of court.

Charles Suffolk was happy to be ambassador extraordinary for the coronation because he was always anxious to please the king and so remain in the royal favour. He felt quite confident that, as he had had no contact at all with Mary recently, he was completely out of peril. He was determined that things should stay exactly as they were.

On the coronation morning, Charles was fetched from his lodgings by the Duke of Montmorency and conducted to one of the seats of honour reserved for ambassadors in the sanctuary by the High Altar and very near the queen. Louis had no official place in the ceremony so he watched everything from a small closet window.

The new Queen of France was escorted into the great cathedral by Francis, Duc de Valois, walking in a stately manner behind the famous ducal names of France carrying on cushions the coronation regalia. Kneeling before the altar, Mary was anointed by Cardinal de Pré with Holy Oil, repeating after him the prescribed prayers and vows. She received the sceptre and the symbol of justice. The cardinal put the traditional ring on her finger as a sign of her marriage with the land of France. Finally, he placed the immense crown of Jeanne of Navarre on her head. Francis then advanced to her side and handed her to the Chair of State. Very soon the queen began to feel the crown an impossible weight and the duke, to relieve her, then lifted it and held it above her head for the remainder of the ceremony. That morning it was natural that all eyes were on the queen as the central figure, and it would be true to say that the assemblage was entranced by her bearing and charm. Many pitied her for being forced to marry such a senile husband. But Mary did not seem to pity herself, for she had begun to appreciate the great kindness the king showed her in private as well as in public.

The queen received Holy Communion at the High Mass which followed. The cathedral choir sang their thousand-year-old Gregorian chants. It was a perfect day.

After resting in her private apartments, Mary gave an audience in the afternoon to the ambassadors and in the evening a special one to ambassador extraordinary the Duke of Suffolk and his suite in her salon.

Early the next morning, Louis left for Paris so that he would be able to receive her personally at the entrance to the city. Mary left St Denis a few hours afterwards, lunching at a village en route to time her state entry for the afternoon. On arrival at the city boundary, she found a long procession drawn up and waiting for her. She was to ride quite alone in an open carriage upholstered in gold cloth, the two white horses resplendent with silver harness. Mary had chosen a crown of magnificent pearls, but as a contrast her neck, arms and bust were covered with sparkling gems. Her military escort consisted of the Scotch Guard of Archers and the German Guard, both of which formed part of the French King's bodyguard. Duke Francis rode before the carriage accompanied by other princes of the blood royal: Alençon, Bourbon, Vendôme, Longueville.

Royalty had to accept cheerfully those very slow processions which continually stopped for various deputations and organisations to offer congratulations and addresses of loyalty and all kinds of presents. Mary's gracious smile never faltered: everyone received warm thanks - Wool Merchants, Judges, Lawyers, Professors and Students of the University of Paris, Bakers, Wine Sellers.

It was dark when the queen's carriage drew up at Notre Dame Cathedral, illuminated in her honour. Mary made her "offering" before the High Altar and was then escorted by torch bearers along the river bank to the palace of the Conciergerie, on the way visiting the superb shrine of the Sainte Chapelle. Not surprisingly, poor Louis was in a state of complete exhaustion by now and retired to his palace of Tournelles.

But for Mary, the long day had not finished, for she had to change her "toilette" to preside at a long state banquet. Claude, Duchess of Valois, was present, as well as all the other royal ladies. It was fashionable in the France of the time for elaborate "subtleties" to be served on grand occasions. A subtlety was moving food - the moving was done by clockwork. It was placed in motion on the table before the guests were served and that was done while it was in movement, or when the clockwork mechanism had stopped. It was all very childish and pretentious but very popular.

The food (usually vegetables, sweets or pastry) was moulded in the shape of perhaps a wing of the wire frame of a bird which flapped its wings. Others, more sophisticated, might be two animals or two soldiers fighting. After the meal the machinery was washed and re-used. No royal banquet seemed to be complete without some of these novelties although they could not have added to the flavour of the food.

The next morning, the queen attended an official High Mass followed by a City of Paris reception. Then she drove to the Palais de Tournelles to visit her husband, who was still in bed recovering from his exertions.

No festivities were complete without jousting in the lists. The jousts honouring the king's nuptials were looked forward to with special excitement as Charles Brandon, Duke of Suffolk, was a famous horseman and jouster. Rides were arranged by one contestant challenging another. Right at the beginning, Francis challenged Suffolk and the Marquess of Dorset, and was accepted. The king and queen received an ovation when they arrived: Mary sat in the royal box, while Louis was too weak to do anything but recline on a sofa.

The duke won thirteen courses and lost two, while the marquess won most of his rides. Francis, on the other hand was wounded in the hand by an opponent's lance and was obliged to withdraw from the lists. The queen showed openly that she favoured the English combatants and delighted in their success. So indeed did Louis, probably because he had a profound dislike of his heir. As if to prove that this was a dangerous sport, two Frenchmen were killed in that day's jousting.

Towards the end of the day Francis chose to play a dirty trick, taking a risk in breaking one of the first rules of the sport. He disguised a big German as a French knight and put him in the lists. Suffolk at the first course floored the German, the tip of his lance entering his opponent's visor. The judges stopped the contest when blood flowed through the perforation but the German did not dare show his face so he had to be ignominiously smuggled away from the field.

Mary had been a queen for only a short time when she realised that she lacked reliable people to advise her on French royal customs and provide her with inside knowledge of the king's health and his likes and dislikes. She asked for help from the permanent English embassy, but nobody had sufficient experience to assist her. Eventually, a kind of committee was appointed, comprising the Bishop of St Pol, the Governor of Normandy, Brezé and the Duc de Longueville (who by now knew Mary very well). The arrangement proved to be an excellent one and the queen profited greatly from their advice.

One thing the queen could not adjust to at the French court, and was determined to change, was the time of meals. Louis had lived to the timetable of breakfast at seven, lunch (dinner) at ten and dinner (supper) at six p.m. all his life, and had no wish to alter, but his wife managed to persuade him to put back all meals three hours. After a few days the king expressed his pleasure at the new arrangement.

One very bad habit of the court, which ruined all appetites, was the continuous appearance of trays loaded with a great choice of little meat and fish pies and very sweet small cakes. These snacks were served with spiced wine (frequently hot). It is not surprising that, after years of this, some courtiers became heavy drinkers and some, without any doubt, were alcoholics. This custom almost guaranteed that much food was wasted at lunch and dinner, and it was a common sight for full plates to be taken away untouched or merely toyed with.

Served daily were truly gargantuan meals of perhaps more than twenty courses - meals sometimes lasting for hours with a kind of floor show at intervals. Different sorts of game were served as different courses - likewise meat or fish. To ring the changes, fish and meat or fish and game were cooked separately but appeared on the same plate. Cheese was rarely on the menu, but dessert frequently consisted of cake or elaborate concoctions of sugar icing - often accurate models of castles or churches. Many dishes were cooked in beer or wine or laced with spirits.

A large amount of royal and diplomatic correspondence of the 16th century has survived, despite the destruction of monasteries in England and France and the sacking of French palaces and chateaux. The following two samples are informative and mirror the period.

From Henry to Louis:

We have heard how she conducts herself towards you in all humility and reverence so that you are well content with her and we have conceived very great joy, pleasure and content understanding this. All our will, pleasure and intention is that in so acting she should persevere from good to better if she wish and desire to have our love and fraternal benevolence and thus we gave her advice and counsel before her departure from us and we make no doubt that you will, day by day, find her more and more all that she ought to be to you and that she will do everything which will be to your will, pleasure and contentment.[4]

From the English Ambassador, the Earl of Worcester, to Thomas Wolsey, Archbishop of York:

My Lord, I assure you that King Louis has a marvellous mind to content and please his Queen and is devising new collars and goodly gear for her. He showed me the goodliest and richest sight of jewels that ever I saw. I would never have believed it if I had not seen it for I assure you all that ever I have seen is not to compare to the fifty five great pieces that I saw of diamonds and rubies and seven of the greatest pearls that I have ever seen besides a great number of other goodly diamonds, rubies and enormous pearls. The worse of the second sort of stones be priced and cost two thousand ducats. Of the principal stones there has been refused for one of them one hundred thousand ducats. And when he had showed me all he said that all should be for his wife. Another coffer also was there that was full of goodly girdles, collars, chains, bracelets, beads of gold and other divers goodly jewels. I make no doubt but she shall have a good life with him by the grace of God.[5]

While official correspondence followed that pattern, courtiers had a field day with endless coarse jokes about the royal couple. Whispered asides and smirks were the order of the day. Both Francis and his mother, Louise of Savoy, let it be known that they were convinced that there would be no fruit of the union.

Soon after her coronation, the queen began to receive complaints and lamentations from members of her suite, who had been dismissed by Louis at Abbeville and sent back to England to find that their requests to King Henry for indemnity were ignored. For some of these people this was a disaster, for they had no resources to fall back on. People who had spent all they had on new clothes and those who had incurred debts were particularly in distress. Mary was shattered at reading some of the letters, so being charitable and kind-hearted the matter was not ignored. All her life Mary cared for her servants. She now arranged with her jeweller, William Verner of London, to present her afflicted ones with a piece of jewelry each, which had to be shown at court as proof that they had been reimbursed by Mary the Queen. Lady Guildford received a very special gift as she had given outstandingly devoted service over many years.

Louis seemed to be rejuvenated by the coming of a young wife. He wore a happy expression; he enjoyed his meals and the new timetable of serving. The couple were staying at the chateau of St Germain-en-Laye not far from the capital, where the king thought he was able to hunt again and enjoy once more indoor games and even dancing. Alas, it was wishful thinking, for he had to remain resting in the country while his queen returned to Paris alone for more official receptions and formal engagements. He accepted her absence on royal business although he missed her when away. Louis loved to have her company, especially when she played the lute and sang for him.

Ever since landing in France, Mary wrote constantly to her brother with requests - many of them quite trivial and it was not long before Henry gave up answering. She then turned to Wolsey, and a stream of letters came to him asking for her demands to be passed on to the king. She never seemed to understand that both men had their own complicated affairs to worry about - much more important than her tiny problems which were not really problems at all.

In spite of King Louis' high spirits, courtiers noted that he was going downhill, and that his marriage had really led to a deterioration. Every day, unkind remarks were made about his health, and everyone gave freely an opinion of how long remained to him on this earth. Every day, the king presented his queen with more beautiful precious stones, mostly unset. Every day, he made her touching compliments and praised her conduct and looks to his visitors. He had intense pride that this ethereal beauty belonged to him, and spoke as though she was a vision and not real. The pathetic and touching relationship of this strange marriage was funny to outsiders but intense and real to both Louis and his wife.

The king returned to his Palais de Tournelles in Paris for Christmas, but the usual celebrations were curtailed because of his illness. King and Queen spent much time quietly together taking pleasure in each other's company as though they both refused to believe that it could not last a great deal longer. Just after Christmas he wrote with his own hand a letter to Henry VIII, telling that the queen "daily conducts herself towards me in such sort that I know not how to praise her and I ever more love, honour and hold her dear."[6] The letter is dated 28th December and it was the last letter he wrote.

The last day of 1514 saw a terrible storm strike Paris with thunder and torrents of rain. Great damage was done to buildings and many in the city were in fear. The storm went on and on, and during it, early on the first day of 1515, His Most Christian Majesty Louis XII of France died suddenly, leaving his eighteen-year-old widow, the Dowager Queen Marie of France, deeply, though surprisingly, in sorrow.

Chapter Five

To conform with tradition as Dowager Queen, Mary at once dressed completely in the mourning colour of white and so for that sad period was known as "La Reine Blanche". Again, in accordance with custom, she retired to the seclusion of the small Hôtel de Cluny, so called because of its neighbour, a religious house of the Cluniac order. The little palace had been built in Paris by Cardinal Amboise a few years previously.

The usual elaborate mourning was decreed for the king who lay in state in the palace of Tournelles with all his royal regalia. A long procession of troops, civil dignitaries, organisations, all in full mourning, passed through streets with buildings draped in black to escort their sovereign on his last journey for the Requiem Mass at Notre Dame. Louis was buried, as he wished, by the side of his wife, Anne of Brittany.

Although Francis de Valois had succeeded as Francis I, it was not known whether Mary was pregnant, and proof of this was needed to ensure proper succession to the throne and permit a coronation. If Mary did have a posthumous son, he would be king and a long regency would become necessary. To avoid any possible trickery and a conception caused by someone other than Louis, his mother, Louise of Savoy, at once took precautions and had a close watch kept day and night on the Dowager Queen Mary. To discover the position as early as possible, Francis began calling daily on the secluded widow, and this conduct embarrassed her for she knew very well that he was a womaniser. The king refrained from asking a blunt question, but he put it in another way when he announced that his wife, the new Queen Claude, was expecting the joy of motherhood and enquired whether a like happiness was hers. Mary answered that Francis I was the only King of France. This was the answer that Francis had been praying for, and he left to begin arrangements for his coronation.

Whenever Francis saw a beautiful woman he wanted her and at once tried to possess her by means fair or foul. This was no secret, for he did not take the trouble to hide his adventures. From the first time he had seen Mary at Abbeville, the kiss and pressure on her hand told her everything. Now she was a widow and totally without protection, in seclusion and so without her male household. A Dowager Queen had to stay in mourning retirement for forty days and Mary's fears began to grow. Francis had now been told what he wanted to know and so there was no reason for further visits, but his daily calls continued. He then dismissed all her English ladies and appointed some French Maids of Honour as substitutes. These he asked to withdraw whenever he came. Understandably, Mary was in a panic, expecting every moment that he would lose control and rape her. She was quite alone with him and out of earshot of her attendants (who would not have come to her assistance anyway as the king was involved). She had heard so much about the king's numerous conquests she knew for certain that he had no feeling for his women and she could not rely on his chivalry.

Mary felt abandoned, for if she escaped one trap, she would fall into another. Besides pestering the Dowager Queen to become his mistress, Francis was strongly urging her to marry one of the several candidates he favoured for political motives - it was the old story cropping up again. If she avoided that proposal, she knew that once back in England her brother would not feel in the slightest bit bound by his promise to allow her a free choice of a second husband.

There was only one man Mary wanted: Charles Brandon, Duke of Suffolk. To make the situation even more complicated, she knew that Charles, although fond of her, would try to avoid marriage because he was frightened of King Henry's violent anger which, at the very least, would mean banishment from court and an end to his position as court favourite. A strong possibility was life imprisonment in the Tower or decapitation. A stark choice indeed.

Mary decided that if Charles could not move, she would. In any case, she must take some action to protect herself from the violence of Francis. The matter was urgent.

At this point it is necessary to say that the late King Louis in various asides to courtiers hinted that, in spite of appearances, he had consummated the marriage. Most courtiers believed that this was not the case and that the ancient bridegroom was merely boasting. Their belief was confirmed, they thought, by the queen, who wore her hair in a style which usually indicated virginity. That was the situation when the king died. Did it have any bearing on the new king's open courtship of the widow? Given his habits it was extemely likely.

As if coping with Francis was not enough, Mary was now receiving from Wolsey her brother's firm order not to promise herself in marriage to anyone. Cooped up in the small palace and seeing nobody except Francis and her maids, she became desperate and hardly knew what she was doing but, cornered as she was, she had to do something.

Meanwhile, back in London, the news of the death of the French king created an upset and uncertainty. At court the great question was whether Mary was pregnant. If so, would she give birth to a male who would be the infant King of France? Charles Brandon had returned to London in November having accomplished his mission to the French court to congratulate Louis on his marriage and Mary on her coronation. Official Masses for the soul of Louis were celebrated in London and Brandon was ordered to return to France to represent Henry at the funeral of Louis and to express his sympathy with his sister on the loss of her husband.

King Henry was now thinking how to get Mary back to England in order to arrange a second profitable political marriage for her. Francis was also considering what marriage he could make for the Dowager Queen of France which would bring the best political advantage to his country.

Henry and Wolsey feared that Francis would forbid Mary's return to England. The idea of possible rape of the queen by the new king crossed both their minds, given his reputation, and neither knew then that he had taken to visiting her quite alone and without attendants. There was a danger that Francis would send the Dowager Queen to a provincial castle and isolate her from the English household. She might even be imprisoned or placed under house arrest.

Almost every unmarried royal personage in Europe was being considered, as kings put out feelers for their particular candidate. Mary's ex-fiancé, Charles of Castile had been proposed, as well as his agèd grandfather, the Emperor Maximilian.

Both kings were unscrupulous and both wanted to use Mary as a pawn. And she was fully aware of the danger, having lived in a court all her life.

One of her letters to King Henry read:

For the furtherance of your affairs you moved me to marry with my lord and late husband King Louis of France, whose soul God pardon, though I knew he was very agèd

59

and sickly yet for the advancement of the said peace and for the furtherance of your causes I was contented to conform myself to your said notion so that if I should fortune to survive the said late king I might with goodwill marry myself at my liberty without your displeasure. Wherefore, good brother, you condescended and granted as you well know promising me that in such case you would never provoke or move me but as mine own heart and mind should be best pleased and that wheresoever I should dispose myself you would wholly be contented with the same. And upon that your good comfort and faithful promise I assented to the said marriage else I would never have granted to as at the same time I showed unto you more at large.[7]

In 1514, King Henry elevated Brandon to the Dukedom of Suffolk and, to help him to support that high rank, gave him the confiscated East Anglian estates of Edmund de la Pole - previous Duke of Suffolk - who had been executed for treason. Later, Brandon added lands on the Welsh borders also previously owned by the de la Pole family. Even so, Brandon never had enough money and all his life he was in debt in spite of being one of England's largest landowners. For that reason he resented being sent on his first mission to France for Mary's coronation, the cost of which put him deeper in the red. When the king asked him to go on a second mission to represent the English king at the funeral of Louis, Charles Brandon was still more displeased, for he would be put to yet more expense. Furthermore, he was not sure how much the king knew about his flirtation with his sister, neither was he sure that Mary would not be indiscreet - if indeed she still loved him - and so damage his relationship with Henry. In any case, the duke hated absenting himself from court being always nervous that another would step into his shoes as the king's favourite.

At this time, Warham, Archbishop of Canterbury, had been Chancellor of England for nearly ten years. It was an arduous job and Warham a weak man in declining health. For some time Wolsey, Archbishop of York, had been gradually taking over these duties while Warham slipped into the background. Ambitious and thoroughly capable, Wolsey was encouraging Canterbury's retirement, and continued to do so by making himself indispensable to the king and his Council. In 1516, the Archbishop of York achieved his ambition and became the Chancellor, until his downfall in 1529.

Knowing that Wolsey constantly had the ear of her royal brother, Queen Dowager Mary wrote to the proud and clever archbishop answering his letter transmitting Henry's order to her not to re-marry in France but to return to England:

My own good Lord,
I pray you as my trust is in you, for to remember me to the king my brother, for such causes and business as I have for to do. For as now I have no other to put my trust in but the king and you and as it shall please the king and his council I will be ordered. And so I pray you, my lord, to show his grace - seeing that the king my husband is departed to God (whose soul God pardon). And whereas you advise me that I should make no promise, my lord, I trust the king my brother and you will not reckon me in such childhood. I trust I have so ordered myself since I came hither that I trust it hath been to the honour of the king, my brother. If there be anything that I may do for you I would be glad to do it in these parts. No more to you at this time, but Jesus preserve you.
Written at Paris the 10th day of January 1515.
To my Lord Archbishop of York.[8]

She followed this with a letter to Henry in the same strain now begging him to send for her as she was constantly receiving requests inconsistent with her honour. At the same time, she resolved that the next time Francis visited she would stake her future in a most desperate appeal to him as a Prince of the blood royal and tell him of her love secret. Whatever happened she could not be in a worse plight than she was at that moment.

When Francis visited the following day and, as usual, dismissed her attendants, Mary knelt before him and refused to rise. She begged him, as she always did, not to make any more advances nor speak any more about possessing her. She asked him to promise not to molest her or take her by force. She then said she would tell him her love secret and invited him not to reveal it on his word as a true prince.

The royal widow then told him that she and Suffolk had been promised to each other long before she came to France and that they had established a secret code for communication adding that her brother had not been told. She waited for the thunder to begin.

To her amazement, the king at once pleasantly agreed to help to achieve her desire and told her he would write to Henry to plead for her. She was so surprised at that sudden reversal of her fortunes she was abject in her thanks and gratitude. Only later did she realise that Francis was advancing his own aims by manoeuvre, neutralising Mary in England and preventing her from being used as an instrument to cement an English alliance with Austria and Spain.

Unknown to Mary or Francis, King Henry had now arranged to send the Duke of Suffolk to Paris on the customary embassy to express condolence on the death of Louis XII and to represent him at the coronation of Francis. Suffolk was to request at the same time the return of the Dowager Queen Mary with her dowry. Wolsey, who had more than a suspicion of Mary's feelings of Brandon, advised Henry to summon his ambassador and make him swear on oath that he "would not abuse his trust nor show any partiality to the young queen consigned to his guardianship" which covered any intimacy between Mary and himself or any proposal of marriage. Suffolk swore the required oath to Henry at Eltham Palace without any hesitation, for he had never had any idea of letting an affair of the heart interfere with his position as court favourite.

Meanwhile, Mary's period of white mourning had passed and she was now able to receive visitors, re-assume the ordering of her household and transact any business required. She was not sorry to see the end of her frustrating seclusion.

One of her first audiences was granted to an English friar who wished to speak privately with her. On admittance he told her that in England there was a strong rumour that she was going to marry the Duke of Suffolk in Paris and, warning her that such an action would be fatal, urged her not to accept such an offer. Mary knew by questioning him that he was an agent of the Duke of Norfolk, who was Suffolk's rival and indeed his enemy at court. After realising the source of the advice, Mary passed no comment on the reason for the visit but angrily dismissed the friar.

A messenger came from the French court, returning from the coronation at Rheims, that the special embassy from Henry had arrived in France but too late for the coronation. However, by quick travelling, Suffolk and his suite caught up with the royal party at Senlis where Francis accorded an audience. The ambassador delivered his formal message of condolence and congratulation to the king, and shortly afterwards Francis summoned Suffolk for a private meeting with him. During the conversation, the king spoke of the Dowager Queen: "Treat the queen as a loving son would his mother." Suffolk formally answered, "My honour will oblige me so to do." The duke wondered at the direction the conversation had taken for he did not know that Mary had confessed to the French king her love secret. Then Francis dropped his bombshell. "My Lord of Suffolk there is rumour that you have come to marry the queen, your master's sister." The envoy went pale with shock realising his perilous position in France as well as England. He managed to retain his diplomatic calm: "I hope your grace will not think me guilty of such madness as to come to a kingdom and marry the queen of that country without the knowledge of the king. It was not so arranged by my master nor by me." Brandon's French was inadequate, but he managed to stumble on and make himself clear to the king, for in such a secret matter as this an interpreter could not be employed.

Francis then stopped the game he was playing with the English envoy and tried to reassure him by disclosing that Mary had already confessed to a secret understanding with him. He also said that he had promised the Dowager Queen that he would do all that he could to bring the romance to a satisfactory conclusion. Francis then dismissed him extending his hand to be kissed as Suffolk dejectedly murmured, "I shall displease my king in this matter." In parting, the king said that both he and Queen Claude would write to Henry pleading for clemency.[9]

The English embassy duly came to Paris and presented itself at the Hôtel de Cluny to express Henry's condolences on the death of Louis to his widow. The Dowager Queen arranged that the audience should take place immediately. Suffolk and his suite entered the audience chamber and began the customary formal speeches, Mary replying in the prescribed manner. Then more profound bows and kneeling. The suite noticed that Francis had permitted the queen's English ladies to rejoin her service. The ambassador then spoke of Henry's explicit instructions to her - that she must not marry again and must not remain in France. Mary answered that she could not wait to see her belovèd brother again. The embassy then prepared to leave when, unexpectedly, the Queen motioned that Suffolk should remain alone with her. The surprised suite and also Mary's female attendants retired.

Greatly embarrassed at being alone with Mary, Suffolk waited in respectful silence until royalty spoke. Mary also waited. Feeling increasingly nervous, Brandon began by enquiring respectfully and in courtly language whether the French King had been kind to her. At the same moment Mary burst into a pent-up torrent of tears and sobs and in an almost incoherent outpouring of words attempted to describe Francis' daily unmistakable advances and her increasing fear that some violence would be done her. Her genuine distress brought a responsive emotion in Charles but he forced himself to remember her rank on the dais and under the canopy and his standing on the floor below her. Nobody could remain unaffected at the sight of such beauty in extreme misery.

But there had to be one cool head, and Charles attempted to tell her than any danger from King Francis had now passed and he felt sure that King Henry would not go back on his promise to allow his sister to choose freely her second husband unrestricted by political advantage or by rank.

Feeling a hesitation in Charles' manner, Mary realised that she had to take the initiative. "I will be open with you," she said. She told the duke that she wanted to marry him and indeed would have no other husband but him. "If I went to England I should never be permitted to marry you so if you do not agree to marriage here and now I shall never have you and will never return to England. If I did return I should be sent to Flanders to be married to Charles of Castile because of his rank. Remember I have been married to the highest man in France and the first gentleman of France has courted me. I would rather be torn to pieces than go to Flanders to marry royal Charles."[10] The duke could hardly understand her she was so agitated and convulsed with sobbing.

Suffolk tried earnestly to make her believe that he truly wanted to marry her and suggested that they both should write to Henry seeking permission to marry before proceeding further, and told her of the oath he swore at Eltham Palace. The breaking of such an oath as this would certainly bring down the king's wrath on them both with frightful punishments. He said that the pleading letters of Francis and Claude would help to ensure the consent they needed.

But Mary would have none of this. She would not even hear of writing to her brother, insisting that they must be married first and ask for clemency afterwards: "I would rather die than agree to anything else." Finally it had come to the point when the duke had to decide at that very moment. "If I cannot have my desire and if you will not be content to follow my mind, look never after this day to have the proffer again."

Very much against his will, and frightened of the consequences, Brandon capitulated. It is said that at this moment Louise of Savoy came into the room and seeing the young queen close to hysterics, after being told what had happened, advised the couple to take advantage of a priest beginning Mass in the private chapel of the Hôtel de Cluny. And so, witnesses (all French) being procured, Mary had her so ardent desire. Within the hour they were man and wife.

Chapter Six

The newly-weds the following day were in a state of panic that Henry would take extreme measures against them. They both knew him well. He was very bad tempered when crossed and vindictive. Also he was very greedy. So there was only one thing to do. Mary remembered the vast store of priceless jewelry that the agèd Louis had presented to her in the short space of three months. Her brother was known for his passionate love of precious stones and precious metals. All this delicious hoard was in France and outside Henry's power. Mary decided at once and without hesitation that her vast treasure must all be used as a fabulous bribe to persuade the king to grant clemency and accept the marriage.

Accordingly Mary, now Duchess of Suffolk, wrote in great humility to Henry begging for pardon and recognition of her marriage, at the same time sending him a Deed of Gift of all Louis' presents, but wisely keeping them in her possession until the king agreed to her proposal. The pathetic heavily tear-stained document executed on thick court paper by an obviously agitated hand describes the scene in the Hôtel de Cluny that February morning in 1515:

A Bill of Gift Made by the French Queen of Gold and Jewels Given Her by King Loys

Be it known to all manner of persons that Mary, Queen of France, sister unto the King of England, giveth freely unto the said king my brother all such plate and vessels of gold as the late King Loys of France the XII of that name, gave unto me, the said Mary, his wife. And also by the same presents I do freely gift unto my said brother, King of England, the choice of such special jewels, all that my said

65

lord and husband, King of France, gave. Unto the performance whereof I bind me ... [the rest is illegible due to wetness of the paper].
From Paris, by your loving sister,
Mary, Queen of France.[11]

From then on, Mary and Charles lived together openly in order that matters could be made quite secure and emphasize that theirs was a real marriage.

A few days afterwards, Mary wrote a long and detailed letter to her brother telling him quite truthfully all that had happened during her widowhood: the attempts of Francis to marry her with candidates of his own choosing for some political advantage, and then his repeated pleading his passion for her, her disclosure to him of her secret love when he instantly left off pestering her and "ceased conduct not in accordance with my honour." She hinted that, if there was any question of forcing her into a marriage she did not choose, she might enter a foreign convent where she would not be happy. She took all the blame for her union with Suffolk, saying that she proposed marriage and insisted on an immediate ceremony in spite of Brandon's protest that he would be breaking an oath to his king.

Suffolk in his turn now wrote to Henry and to Wolsey giving both an accurate account of what had happened:

When I came to Paris the queen had me in audience the day after. She said she must be short with me and show to me her pleasure and mind. She said if I would be ordered by her she verily would have none but me. She weeped as never saw I woman so weep.[12]

He also described how Francis had told him that Mary had confessed to her wish to have the duke and none other. In his letter to Wolsey, he said that the marriage had been consummated the night of the wedding and with such strength that it was quite possible that the Queen/Duchess was already with child - this was written deliberately as it made it almost impossible for Henry to have the union repudiated without disgracing his sister.

Francis generously agreed to Mary's taking to England the enormous pile of treasure which she had accumulated through royal presents, including the famous "Mirror of Naples" diamond. Much later, when Queen Claude heard of this, she was furious and sulked for days but it was too late to do anything, for it was already on the other side of the Channel.

When conciliatory letters arrived from the king and Wolsey the Suffolks thought their problems at an end; in great delight Mary Suffolk wrote:

My most kind and loving brother I humbly recommend myself to your grace thanking you entirely for your comfortable letters beseeching your grace most humbly to continue thus towards me and my friends as our special trust is in your grace and that it may please you to send for me that I may shortly see your grace which is the thing that I most desire in this world and I and all mine are at your grace's commandment and pleasure. At Paris the 6th of March by your loving sister Marie.[13]

Wolsey by now was writing to Charles to tell him of the great displeasure of the king and his council that a person of his low birth should be so bold as to aspire to marriage with a royal princess and anointed queen, and hinting that Henry might well dissolve it by separating Suffolk head from Suffolk body. This was the usual Tudor playing of politics which was to put someone in the wrong, always playing hot and then cold. In this way, ammunition was provided against the person which might come in useful in the future.

Mary at once wrote another humble letter. Eventually Wolsey told the couple to leave Paris and proceed to Calais where they were to await further instructions. Accordingly they left the capital with their suites on 18th April.

This wait at Calais was said to be to obtain the approval of the Privy Council to the marriage, but in reality that council was the king's tool and it did exactly as he wished. Nevertheless, Mary was obliged to write an extremely long letter which went into great detail for the third or fourth time. She carefully emphasized the king's promise to allow her to choose her second husband. She ended -

Now that God had been pleased to call my said late husband to His Mercy and that I am at my liberty, dearest brother, remembering the great virtues that I have seen in my Lord of Suffolk to whom I have always been of good mind, as you well know, I have been clearly determined to marry with him and I assure this came from my own mind without any request of my said Lord of Suffolk or any other persons. To be plain with your grace I have so bound myself to him that for no cause earthly I will or may change from the same. So my good and most kind brother

67

I now beseech your grace to take this matter in good part and to give to me and my Lord of Suffolk your good will.[14]

A stream of abject and flattering letters now went from Mary to her brother. An example:

And now that your grace knows the two offences of the which I have been the only occasion I most humbly and as your most sorrowful sister require you to have compassion upon us both and to pardon our offences and that it will be please your grace to write to me and to my Lord of Suffolk some comfortable words for it will be of the greatest comfort to us both.

By your loving and most humble sister - Mary.[15]

From the English territory of Calais, Mary wrote to her brother yet again, to confirm her intention of giving her French presents to him, although as a precaution she had not brought the treasure with her but left it in a secret place on the other side of the frontier. The greed and injustice of taking his young sister's gifts from her late husband shows how wildly extravagant was his court: he was now almost permanently short of funds, having squandered the whole of the vast fortune left by his father only six years previously.

At the beginning of May, Wolsey wrote, giving Henry's permission for the couple to proceed to England, and on a lovely spring morning they made the crossing with the sea like a lake. Mary had the whole of the collection of gold and jewelry in her luggage - "my winnings in France" as she often described them. After being received by the king and queen with great affection at the Palace of Greenwich, the Suffolks went through a second ceremony of marriage in the Franciscan chapel which adjoined.

The festivities were enormously expensive, as always on these occasions, with immense quantities of food and drink being consumed (and wasted). Fancy dress balls and jousting were greatly enjoyed by these young folks. Charles Suffolk was already in debt to the crown when he was asked to pay the bill for all these wedding amusements. He had imagined that, as he had married the king's sister, he would be excused payment but Wolsey had other ideas and insisted on receiving the money. This caused sharp words between the two men, which led to a permanent coldness between them. It was to have grave consequences for Wolsey some fourteen years afterwards.

✿ ✿ ✿

When Mary left Greenwich for France, she saw the idle fleet stripped bare, riding at anchor in the river. When she returned nearly a year later, it was still there waiting for the next war with France. There were twenty to thirty ships in the laid-up fleet but the largest (*MARY ROSE* and *HENRI GRACE A DIEU*) were easily distinguishable from the shore. All were now lifeless and already shabby. The happy newly-married Queen/Duchess perhaps hardly gave a thought to her ship, as it was the custom to neglect the navy completely between wars.

🌹 🌹 🌹

After an enjoyable stay at court, the Suffolks went down to the country to inspect their vast estates of wild poor land and their scattered manor houses and castles. At once Mary found a favourite home - Westhorpe Hall - which remained a chosen retreat for the rest of her life. She loved this part of the country at first glance, and from then on took a great interest in the workers and the agèd poor for whom she built some alms houses.

In July, the Queen/Duchess found she was pregnant which made her very happy. In February of the next year, Queen Katherine gave birth to a daughter, later Queen Mary I of England. The baby was named after her aunt, the Duchess of Suffolk. A few months later, the Suffolks had a son, Henry, who was named after the king. Some years afterwards he was created Earl of Lincoln.

Mary had lived at the very centre of court life until now and was delighted to be far from the formality of palaces. Nevertheless, being royal, she had her official household of ladies and gentlemen in attendance. She was also royal in that she had no idea at all of money, and although wealthy, she had many calls on her purse and was always in debt. In this her husband was exactly like her, but was constantly worried at owing vast sums. Most of their income was wasted - they owned many large houses which, even though skeleton staffs only were resident, were a great drain. These houses were seldom, if ever, visited and then only for hunting. They also had properties in Herefordshire which they never saw. Suffolk Place in London was a huge rambling riverside palace and they owned another residence in Stepney.

When obliged to be at court, Mary much preferred to live in Suffolk Place than her suite in the royal palace where the king was staying at the moment. She had a permanent suite in Greenwich, Richmond, Windsor and perhaps several others. Each suite had to be paid for whether used or not.

The Suffolk town house, Suffolk Place, was on the south bank of the Thames opposite the city of London. Although there were buildings on that bank, it was considered country by Londoners. The mansion was surrounded by extensive and well kept gardens in the formal Tudor style and the large estate consisted chiefly of a forest of oaks. Access to the north bank was easy as the famous London Bridge was nearby. Adjacent to the river, Suffolk Place had its own private quay and, of course, private Suffolk barges for transport to any of the royal palaces. The south bank roads were less well maintained even than those on the north bank - hence reliance on the river.

The house itself was built round a courtyard and was considered very elegant. It could accommodate a large number of guests as well as a small army of servants. A great feature was the large picture gallery with its walls lined with portraits (this was very fashionable) and a magnificent great hall used for dining, receptions and dancing.

As the house was so convenient to the capital, Mary could entertain large numbers of the élite who could return home by bridge or barge the same day and so obviate the necessity of staying the night. Here came from time to time King Henry and Queen Katherine (still very close friends with Mary), as well as Wolsey, foreign visiting royalty, ambassadors to the English court, archbishops and bishops and members of the great English nobility. London has long since swallowed up the whole of the large Suffolk Place estate and no trace remains of the house.

Mary always regarded Westhorpe as her real home. It was not a palace but an extremely large manor house surrounded by a moat. For the duchess, the estate was the great attraction, being mostly wild, poor land little cultivated. Here she could relax with her children and patronize local events like country fairs and religious feast days. On these occasions, she brought her own grand tent and held court, receiving in state East Anglian notables. It may well be that the number of attendants and servants kept at Westhorpe Hall was governed by the size of the building, but it was considered that the standard of living there for the Duke and Duchess was extemely modest and certainly much below the level for royalty.

For some now unknown reason, the house was demolished in the eighteenth century and no doubt some of the stones were used to construct a farmhouse nearby. The moat bridge remains and also the Dowager Queen's coat of arms over the doorway of the present farmhouse. The small parish church (where the Brandons heard Mass when not attending

Westhorpe private chapel) still stands, after six centuries of use, and an important-looking pew is said to be the one the French Queen occasionally used.

In November of 1515, the Papal Protonotary arrived in England, bringing the Cardinal's Red Hat which was given to the Archbishop of York, Thomas Wolsey, at a ceremony in Westminster Abbey. Always a proud man, his raising to the cardinalate went to Wolsey's head, and his show of opulence became greater and greater. He used much gold-decorated furniture and the Red Hat was always carried before him by a servant so that nobody could forget his importance. Courtiers realised that Wolsey was aiming at the Papal Throne. Many were jealous of his power in England, for the king was still friendly towards him. Henry appreciated his remarkable organising ability and outstanding memory, but his high position, as always, depended on the king's whim.

Wolsey and the Privy Council reminded the Suffolks from time to time that they should make some payment towards the reduction of their huge debts, but the couple made only token economies, leaving the expensive holes in their purses wide open as before. Occasionally they entertained the king at one of their houses, and in those days this was a truly colossal expense, but an honour which could not be refused.

As if this were not enough, Henry suddenly demanded a payment of twenty-four thousand pounds to cover Mary's marriage expenses in 1514 when she married Louis in France. The demanded immediate settlement was not possible so a compromise was agreed - payment by instalments. The Duke and Duchess found even the instalment system a great burden and indeed often failed to meet these obligations. Sometimes the debts grew instead of diminishing, so that both acquired permanent status of debtors to the Crown. But they never made any real attempt to stop incredible extravagance and waste. As could have easily been foreseen, even their funerals were almost completely paid for by the king.

Mary spent much time alone in the country because Charles quickly became restless there and longed for the activity of the court, the goings from one palace and the comings to another, the music, the banquets, the dances, contrived amusements and dangerous political manoeuvres which were so exciting. The scoring of points off enemies and the slight advance or retreat in the favour of a fickle monarch were the very spice of life to Charles Brandon. So adept was he at the game he was almost unique in retaining the goodwill of his sovereign from cradle to grave.

Duke Charles displayed not the slightest interest in his two daughters by his first wife, Lady Anne Browne, and indeed said in no uncertain manner that he did not want to be bothered with them. The kindly stepmother, Mary, thought differently and considered she had a duty towards them. She wanted these motherless girls to stay with her until she was able to find them good husbands. Suffolk reluctantly brought the Lady Anne Brandon home from the court of Margaret of Savoy in the Low Countries where he had placed her. Lady Anne lived happily with her stepmother and then the second daughter, Lady Mary Brandon, joined her. Later Lady Anne was married to Lord Powis and Lady Mary to Lord Monteagle.

The first few days of May were great occasions for celebrating in England for the weather was fresh and warm, which meant the definite end of winter. There was much dancing by young people with meals eaten in the open air. Royalty and courtiers took themselves on horseback to the forests to enjoy folk dancing, picnics and simple rough games which involved chasing ladies who gave mock frightened screams. Formality was abandoned and frolics were the order of the day. Even among the sophisticated it was all very innocent. The Suffolks took much delight in this sort of fun, and king and duke frequently raced each other on their hunters. Once for a joke they requisitioned two huge farm haulage horses and raced them for many kilometres back to Greenwich Palace to amuse the ladies of the court.

Chapter Seven

Mary had led a reasonably happy life, spoilt by her father, indulged by King Louis, loved by her brother in spite of his greed and insensitivity, while she herself had won the husband she dreamed of and became a mother by him. Not so her sister Margaret, the Queen of Scots. She had hardly had a moment of tranquillity since leaving England in 1503 to become the wife of James IV of Scotland. That country had been impossible to govern for centuries. There was perpetual quarrelling and fighting between the great Scottish lairds who were constantly at odds with the crown, as well as with each other. There were murders, kidnappings, skirmishes, and small civil wars. Sides were changed continuously.

From the beginning Margaret had been drawn into these conflicts and she had sent a stream of letters to her father and then her brother, asking for help in her great sufferings. James had always been regularly unfaithful and Margaret was depressed when time passed and there was no sign of pregnancy.

Eventually, in 1506 she gave birth to a son, who died the following year. The queen took an exceptionally long time to recover, and indeed was ill for many months. This was to be the pattern for her future childbeds. When Margaret was eighteen, she gave birth at Holyrood Palace to a daughter who lived only one day. The next year a son was born - he survived nine months.

The king apparently half expected these disasters, thinking them a punishment for the small share he had in his father's murder. James was a religious man and was sorry every time he committed adultery. He really did try to correct his fault, but never had any success. He was kind to all his discarded mistresses, and saw that his numerous illegitimate children were provided for. It was always his intention to make a pilgrimage to Jerusalem in atonement, but his presence was needed constantly in his war-torn country.

Queen Margaret herself went as a pilgrim to a Scottish shrine to petition for a child who would live. Evidently her prayer was heard, for immediately on her return she became pregnant and in April 1512 Prince James of Scotland was born. The baby was so weak and frail that he was not expected to survive, until the wet nurse was changed, after which he slowly picked up strength. Queen Katherine of England had lost her first baby, so Margaret and her small son were still the heirs to the English throne.

Pope Julius II died in 1513 and his successor in the Chair of St Peter was Leo X who excommunicated King James. This was a terrible blow to James, who lived in great anguish thereafter. In the same year, England and Scotland were at war - England being under the regency of Queen Katherine while Henry was away fighting in France, as we described earlier (in Chapter Two).

As a result of James's death in the battle, Margaret became Dowager Queen and her baby son James V of Scotland. During her son's minority, Margaret was to act as regent. She had suffered much ill-health since her marriage but now she rallied and showed unexpectedly much energy. She appeared to be indifferent to the fate of her husband's corpse which was taken by the English army to Richmond and (as an excommunicate) never buried.

At that time, the queen was four months pregnant and, aware that she was always very ill at childbirth, she took steps to ensure the succession of her baby son by arranging his coronation as King of Scotland at Scone. Given the almost permanent unrest in Scotland she feared for her son if she died.

In April 1514, a son was born, christened Alexander, and was given the title, Duke of Ross. For the first time after childbed, Margaret felt in good health and returned to Perth with her two small sons, holding court there. Courtiers began to remark that the nineteen-year-old Earl of Angus was in constant attendance on the Queen Regent. The reason for this was discovered in the August of that year, when it became public knowledge that Margaret had married the young earl secretly the previous month. Angus was completely inexperienced in court life and politics, but at twenty-four the regent was desperately in love with him and, what was more serious, she agreed with everything he said or did.

This rash union immediately caused endless violence and

many people wished to relieve the queen of her regency. The vital interests of the two infant princes were often in the balance as Margaret tried to defend them. The Scottish nobility and clan chiefs took sides, and England, along with other countries, interfered and caused added unrest. Sporadic fighting occurred all over the country. Margaret's two small sons were kidnapped. In the centre of all this incredible chaos, the extent of which had had not been known even in Scotland, the Queen Regent became pregnant. Small wonder that the court thought she was going mad, for she frequently had hysterics and long fits of crying. Eventually her sons were restored to her and she was able to pull herself together and take charge again as regent. But now she had another serious problem - she found herself without any money and there was nobody to make a loan. Her bodyguard was drifting away as she had no funds to pay them.

Her sons were then snatched a second time, to her infinite despair. The disturbances then reached such a pitch (the boys were now in charge of a Frenchman, the Duke of Albany, who was governing the country) that she was in great danger if she remained in Scotland. With the Earl of Angus, she fled across the border managing to reach Morpeth Castle in time to give birth to a daughter. Once again the queen was terribly ill and unable to leave her bed. She wrote to her brother begging for his help.

And Henry was touched by this catalogue of woes. Even he, selfish as he was, could not ignore the sufferings of a sister lying in a cold and draughty castle, ill and weak after a difficult confinement, penniless. Margaret had aleady appealed to some European courts for assistance, complaining of the bad treatment she had received in Scotland and stressing that she was an anointed queen. She was offered much sympathy but no money.

But the queen had still more to endure. In December 1515 she learned that her second son, Alexander, Duke of Ross had died. Already very weak and bedridden, she collapsed when given this news and her attendants thought that she would die. It was rumoured in Scotland that the little prince had been murdered, but this she always rejected for she was certain that the Duke of Albany, who was in charge of the royal children, would not be capable of such a deed.

Following on that sorrow was yet another. Her much loved husband the Earl of Angus became a less frequent visitor to Morpeth Castle. He became bored with the company of his wife who, it must be admitted, hardly made a light-hearted partner after all the troubles she had lived through. Margaret discovered that the earl had found a mistress in the beautiful Lady Jane Stuart of Traquair. He had always been unhappy at being a refugee from Scotland and wanted to regain his estates which had been seized by the crown. Eventually he made up his mind to return to Scotland and make his peace with the Duke of Albany even though he had a capture price on his head. The neglected queen was distraught and wept ceaselessly for the great love of her life - the young and handsome Angus.

The Dowager Queen now had nobody except her newly-born daughter. Her son was held as a prisoner in Scotland by her political enemies. Her own health was so precarious that she found it difficult to leave her bed. Understandably, she was deeply depressed. Henry had written that he was prepared to receive her, and she had no choice but to accept, although she had few illusions about his interest in her. She knew that she would be used as a political weapon against Scotland - the permanent enemy of England.

In April 1516, Margaret set off on her journey south, stopping often to rest as concession to her weakness. As the ever-resilient queen travelled, her health began to improve and her spirits rose at the thought of having some peace in the company of Katherine the Queen and the Queen/Duchess Mary. For the first time since leaving England she would be having some fun - she had been through so much and was only twenty-seven.

At York, to her surprise, the Earl of Angus caught up with her having changed his mind, yet again, and wishing to become part of a Scottish Embassy to King Henry. Did Margaret take him back? Of course she did and without any conditions.

The queen reached Tottenham in May, where Henry was waiting with a large entourage to welcome her with great joy to escort her to the city of London. She had been allocated the enormous mediaeval riverside pile, Baynard's Castle, as a residence. It was a gloomy and forbidding place, like its neighbour, the Tower. But it did not matter: she was home again and there was much embracing and gaiety and spring sunshine and dancing. Besides this, King Henry, who normally had no time for babies, made a great fuss of his small niece dangling her on his knee and singing loudly to her.

Henry and the three queens had great fun that happiest of summers. Court formality was kept to a minimum and many excursions were made into the forests and many meals taken in the open air. Richmond, Greenwich and Windsor rang to the happy laughter of young royalty. It was as if they all knew that this felicitous time could not last and would not be repeated. It was a second innocence. Even Wolsey undid the purse strings on the order of the king and supplied money to Margaret although he made it clear it was a loan and not a gift.

❀ ❀ ❀

News from France showed that King Francis had embarked on a large programme of warship construction, and this irritated Henry, who stepped up plans for a great increase in the English fleet, which had begun over a year before. Some of the ships were huge and therefore expensive. The biggest of this batch of men o'war was the *VIRGIN MARY* which carried two hundred guns and hundreds of soldiers. The king went to Greenwich for the commissioning. Charles and Mary Suffolk had been staying in the country but returned to court for these ceremonies, occupying their suite in the palace. Mary named the warship in French *LA PUCELLE MARIE.*

Besides this new fleet lay the old one, stripped of armament and crews and naturally deteriorating in spite of the retention of sailors for maintenance. There lay the Queen/Duchess's own ship the *MARY ROSE* and the "Great Harry" whose formal name was the *HENRI GRACE A DIEU*, as well as several others of the king's fleet.

The French Ambassador Bapaume was staying at Greenwich at the time and enquired of Suffolk and Wolsey what was the meaning of building more ships when there was already laid up in the river a large fleet which could be put into service very quickly. The Ambassador suggested to Suffolk that his king wanted another war with France, and was enlarging his navy for that purpose.

The duke had a ready answer. "Not at all," he said, "these ships are built to be used as pleasure craft by Queen Katherine and the French Queen Mary." It was an obvious lie which did not deceive Bapaume. The two queens had already dined on the *VIRGIN MARY*, the most recently commissioned ship, which had a large kitchen and dining space for the entertainment of royalty. Eating aboard was considered a novelty much to be enjoyed. When Ambassador Bapaume went on board, he noticed a large quantity of gun powder, which he pointed out to Suffolk, saying it was strange that this was needed on a ship used for pleasure. Nevertheless Duke Charles insisted that the *VIRGIN MARY* had been built for a peaceful purpose knowing, of course, that Bapaume was not hoodwinked and that King Francis would soon receive detailed reports on England's new fleet.

To put the ball in the Frenchman's court Suffolk changed the subject of conversation and enquired why the remainder of the jewelry left behind in France by the Queen/Duchess had not yet been sent and asked him to request his master to forward it without delay. At this time Bapaume wrote to his master that it appeared to him that Wolsey was slipping slightly from his powerful position, for it was noticeable that he was going out of his way to be courteous and complimentary to the Duke and Duchess of Suffolk. This was held to be an indication that Charles Brandon was just as high as ever in the king's favour. It was an accurate assessment, for Henry had recently enjoyed hunting on the Suffolk estates.

Both Queen Katherine and the Queen/Duchess were looking forward to the year 1517, as both were pregnant. Mary had spent the winter in the country, the wild landscape of which she loved. Suffolk disliked the barren uncultivated soil and the flatness. When he was not hunting there he was bored. Mary Suffolk loved the people as well as the land. The peasants were poor and many were in receipt of her charity. The duke had no affection for his tenants and workers and only knew that vast areas on his estate brought in no revenue at all.

In March, Katherine invited the Suffolks to make a pilgrimage with her to Walsingham to ask Our Lady for a good delivery of healthy sons. It was not a hard pilgrimage, but it did entail leaving one's shoes in the Slipper Chapel and walking barefoot for the last two kilometres.

In May, the three queens were together at Richmond Palace to join in the spring revels, when news came from London that there was severe rioting with much destruction of property. This is known to history as the Apprentices' Revolt. It was so alarming that the queens abandoned their plans and returned to the capital. Apparently, it was caused by jealousy of foreigners (principally Spaniards) who had prosperous businesses. Londoners blamed Katherine of Aragon (without any justification) for favouring the Spaniards and obtaining the custom of the court for them. Several rich Spaniards were killed and their houses and shops looted and burnt. A priest in the household of the Duke of Norfolk was killed by a band of these young men, and that duke became involved when he was ordered to quell the disturbance.

Norfolk had only one method of doing this - he hanged about two hundred apprentices by the neck from their masters' shop fronts. Apart from those hanged, the duke had arrested several hundred more who were languishing in prison not knowing their fate.

The mothers of these youths were quite distraught, thinking that their sons would shortly be hanging from a shop sign. They rushed to the palace screaming and shouting so loudly that the noise reached to the queen's apartment. Katherine enquired what the din was all about from some of the women themselves, who were brought to her. Katherine then called Queen Margaret and the Queen/Duchess who were staying at the palace, told them all that had happened and asked them to support her in begging the king for clemency.

The three anointed queens (two of them heavily pregnant) undid their hair, tore and disarranged their clothing. They knelt before the king weeping, and with outstretched arms begged for mercy for the boys, refusing to rise until it had been accorded. At first Henry declined, but later, when the ladies continued to kneel in spite of his command, he gave in and pardoned all the boys in prison. The mothers were delighted and showed their gratitude to each of the royal supplicants. The boys were sent for and knelt before their king in thanksgiving. The crowd cheered. As for Henry, he rode off to Windsor to hunt.

Queen Katherine was again unfortunate in her pregnancy, but in the summer Mary gave birth to a daughter, Frances, at Hatfield House while she was travelling to London. The baby was baptised at Hatfield the sponsors being Katherine and her small child the Princess Mary, for whom Anne Boleyn and Lady Elizabeth Grey stood proxy.

The same summer, Queen Margaret, after a year at the English court, was forced to say farewell to her relatives, for King Henry had patched up his sister's quarrels with her husband, the Earl of Angus, and the Scottish government, who arranged for the Duke of Albany to retire to France. Mary Suffolk was depressed at seeing her sister depart for the country where she had had so many troubles, but there seemed to be some slight chance of peace, now that Albany had gone.

At the border town of Berwick, the earl met his wife with a large escort of troops, and the couple travelled with all speed to Holyrood. Arriving there, the queen ran to her son's room but to her distress was not allowed to see him. The boy king was then spirited away to Craigmillar where eventually Margaret was able to talk to him. But - it is sad to say - the queen's troubles never ended, for the chaos and constant disorder continued until she died in 1541.

In 1518, Charles and Mary went to stay at the royal

mediaeval palace of Woodstock, surrounded by an immense hunting estate. While there, the duchess fell ill of a fever - perhaps the "sweating sickness" contagious and rampant in England at that time. That fever was often fatal so it may be that Mary's illness was not the dreaded one but another with similar symptoms. The court returned to London to greet the arrival of a French delegation which had come to sign the agreement for the proxy marriage between the Princess Mary of England, daughter of Henry, aged two, with the Dauphin of France, son of King Francis I. The Dauphin was still in his cradle.

So the terrible story of infant engagements and proxy marriages continued among royalty in spite of all the misery it caused and in spite of the absence of any practical advantage.

To mark the new rapprochement between England and France Wolsey gave a magnificent banquet. The laden tables looked like those at the feast of a Roman Emperor. Every course was served on gold or silver. Rich presents were given to lady guests and mimes and dancing provided amusement. The villains of the evening's theatricals were pelted with candied fruits by the tipsy diners. It was a party that lasted all night - the king and queen and the Suffolks were guests.

Some days later the duke and duchess felt obliged to return Wolsey's hospitality and gave a banquet - Queen Katherine was eight months' pregnant and so Mary was entertaining for her. Mary's dinner was on a more modest scale than Wolsey's but even so it cost a great deal of money and forced the hosts to retire to the country in order to economise. The Duke and Duchess always did this after a bout of spending but their aim was not achieved, their purses never being replenished. Unfortunately, the Queen's sixth (and last) pregnancy produced a stillborn daughter much to Henry's undisguised and outspoken disappointment.

As a former Queen Consort of France, Mary took part in an entertainment provided for many unfortunate French hostages whose ransoms had not been paid by their families. They had been detained in England since the last war with France and presumably did not stand much chance of release if their families had not been able to raise the ransom money in five years.

Mary spent most of the summer of 1519 at Westhorpe with her young family, with occasional visits to Butley Priory where she was always very happy. Both she and Charles were lay members of the Third Order of Augustinians which was open to the laity. Butley was one of the largest of the English houses of the Augustinians which was perhaps the reason she felt very much at home there. However, these royal visits cost the Priory large sums, because the Brandons always brought a large suite with them who had to be accommodated. At this time Mary and Charles became much more friendly with the king and this caused all of them great satisfaction, for the trio were basically very fond of each other. Henry invited the couple more often to court, which meant almost constant travelling between Westhorpe and London. When at court, of course, Mary and the Duke dined at the High Table, which was the only place she could occupy, being an anointed queen.

Duchess Mary's former fiancé, Prince Charles of Castile, was now Emperor Charles V and still a bachelor. In 1520, Charles V was invited to visit England and Henry did everything that was possible to ensure a warm welcome. The king was at Canterbury and rode through the night to Dover to greet the Emperor and do him honour. The sovereigns liked each other at sight, and enjoyed the short visit of less than a week. King Henry escorted the Emperor to Canterbury where Charles' aunt, Queen Katherine, was waiting to see her nephew for the first time. Mary Suffolk also had never seen him, although she had once been his proxy wife. She was very curious to meet him, but not more so than the courtiers who could hardly contain themselves when the Duchess joined the suite of King and Queen for the various entertainments organised for the great occasion. Emperor and Duchess met shyly and before the eyes of the whole court they greeted each other formally. As far as Charles was concerned, it was obvious that he was enchanted by what he saw. Like everyone who met Mary, he was fascinated by her beauty and began a sulk which lasted throughout his visit. If his mood was not noticed, his dislike of the duke was made very clear. And Mary? As far as anyone could see, she felt nothing at all. While it lasted it was a great titbit for the court gossips.

When the Emperor left for Sandwich to join his ship, the King and Queen with the Duke and Queen/Duchess travelled to Dover with an enormous suite to embark for Calais and from thence to a camp at Ardres to meet King Francis and Queen Claude. This royal encounter is known as the Field of the Cloth of Gold and it was aptly named. Probably the most vulgar and extravagant international conference ever mounted, it accomplished absolutely nothing, for within three years the two nations were at war yet again.

The two queens consort found the gathering boring at first, but the two kings and the Queen/Duchess enjoyed every minute. For Mary, as a woman, it was a triumph. Katherine and Claude later discovered that they had much in common, and became firm friends, spending much time in private conversation in their luxurious tents of expensive highly decorated material. This left Mary very much on her own but the problem was solved as the two kings liked nothing better than galloping great distances on magnificent horses. After the first day the Queen/Duchess was seen riding between them and so she continued, delighting in the exercise. In the camp, she was the second lady of England, and also the second lady of France - a unique situation which had never happened before or since. With a good seat on a horse and eye-catching riding habits, combined with her wonderful looks, she was a sight that most men in the camp remembered throughout their lives. At the numerous banquets, she wore the beautiful dresses that Henry had given her before leaving England, for he was proud of her beauty and wished her to shine in that distinguished company. She would not have been a woman if she had not revelled in the obvious admiration of all those men.

Wolsey was always at hand to talk politics with the French ministers and princes of the blood. He also sang the Masses attended by royalty, who received Holy Communion from his hands.

Neither Katherine or Claude were good dancers and they knew it. Not so Mary. Full of life, she danced every dance in her spectacular gowns of gold and silver thread sewn with jewels. Unfortunately, the Suffolks had to pay for their own enormous suite of clergy, gentlemen and ladies (about fifty of these), numbers of servants for themselves and their suite, and many grooms for nearly a hundred horses. Several of the horses had bejewelled harness and sported curled feathers. All had to be transported across the Channel and back again.

Charles Brandon did not enjoy the camp, as he had to take a back seat in everything except the jousting when, being a born champion at that sport, he relished the ovations he received. But Mary loved it all and hoped it could go on for ever. Typically, neither of them gave a thought to the expense.

When it was all over, the foreign ambassadors reported to their governments and several, including the Venetian envoy, commented on the loveliness and liveliness of the Queen/Duchess contrasting this, in the most ungentlemanly fashion, with the dull plain looks of the ageing queen consort.

The English sovereigns left for Calais vowing lasting friendship with France. Mary hoped very much that this would prove to be so; otherwise, her French revenues would cease, and these were by far the greater part of her income. The money had been paid reasonably regularly by the French but Henry had taken his substantial cut before sending on the remittance to his sister.

The King and Queen, with the Duke and Queen/Duchess, had arranged to entertain the Emperor Charles V in Calais together with his aunt Margaret, Archduchess of Austria. This was the lady who had put Charles Brandon in his place (although she spoke no English and he only very halting French) when, in the company of Henry, he had tried to flirt with her. Unfortunately the entertainment never happened, for a tremendous storm the night before blew open doors and windows of the hall, damaged the roof, destroyed furniture and much of the food.

Henry decided to break the tie so recently made with France, and approached Charles V suggesting a treaty of friendship. Charles responded with enthusiasm and the Anglo-French Alliance was cancelled. Also the engagement between the infant Mary of England and the Dauphin was repudiated and substituted was an engagement between the toddler Mary and the Emperor, aged twenty. This was one of a great many political engagements made by Charles with princesses of several countries and not one of them was consummated. This is possibly one of the worst examples of the futility of child engagements.

The health of the Duchess Mary began gradually to decline after the birth of a second daughter, Eleanor, in 1524, and she constantly complained of a pain in her side. Brandon, still never really happy away from court, spent less and less time with his wife. The four-day journey from Westhorpe to London tired Mary and she was seen at court less frequently and at greater intervals.

About this time, gossip began to spread the the king was enamoured of one of the Queen's Maids of Honour, Anne Boleyn, sister of Mary Boleyn, one of Henry's discarded mistresses. It was rumoured that Anne was ambitious and prone to give herself airs and had even refused Henry as a lover. Although the king continued to show Queen Katherine every respect in public, it was noticed that he avoided her company more and more. Mary was very fond of Katherine and was angry that a queen should be caused distress by her pert, former Maid of Honour, whom she knew well, as Anne had been one of her household during her married life in France.

Mary asked her husband for an explanation of what was

apparently happening at court, and on being told it threatened to be a serious matter, told him she refused to condone her brother's treatment of the queen. Brandon replied sharply that her best course was to remain in the country quietly as the king would brook no opposition to his growing attachment to the Boleyn, and if Henry learned that his sister showed any opposition, Charles himself could be ruined instantly.

At the outbreak of the long expected war with France, the Emperor Charles was staying at Suffolk House as a guest of the Duke and Duchess. He was able to witness the hurried mobilisation of the neglected English fleet in the Thames and among the warships, Mary's own ship the *MARY ROSE*. So Charles V had to cut short his visit, which he was enjoying, and return post-haste to the continent. There he took charge of his army in Italy where it faced the French army under the command of Francis I.

King Henry appointed Brandon to take charge of the English army with the task of invading from Calais. He had some initial successes causing the French heavy casualties, which pleased the king, but then the English suffered bad reverses and had to withdraw to their Calais enclave. This defeat caused the royal temper to explode against Suffolk. Henry only liked winners.

It could not be and was not long before Suffolk returned to favour. The two roisterers were like two peas in a pod, enjoying the same things. Both by now had had several regular mistresses and several illegitimate children whom they loved and provided for after their casual fashion. Mary Boleyn, one of Henry's discarded ladies had now been satisfactorily married off and Katherine thought that this meant that she had heard the last of that family. Because of the war, her sister Anne had returned from France and managed to secure an appointment as Maid of Honour to the queen - a fatal choice. Poor Katherine did not know of the danger for quite a time and when eventually she realised what was happening it was too late. The king and queen had been married for nearly fifteen years and there was still no male heir. Henry's craving for a son became an obsession, and as time passed, he was prepared to sacrifice everything and everybody to achieve his desire.

The Queen/Duchess, now that her husband was abroad with the army, retired to the country with the aim of economising: this was an urgent matter as her French income had stopped. As usual, it turned out to be all talk. In fact, she spent more than ever on enlarging and beautifying the gardens of several of her houses, together with vast sums on reconstructing buildings. She travelled from house to house and entertained lavishly just as before. Money still meant nothing to her and the Suffolk debts grew.

At this time, Mary was extremely worried about a matter which Lady Mortimer had brought up. Lady Mortimer had married Charles Brandon after his marriage had been annulled. It then turned out that his first marriage was valid and should not have been annulled and therefore his marriage with Lady Mortimer was no marriage at all. The lady was now claiming that her marriage to Charles was valid in which case his union with the Dowager Queen of France was invalid. No wonder that Mary was worried for a decision in favour of Lady Mortimer made the Brandon children illegitimate. Quite wisely, Mary put the whole affair before the Pope, and sent all the relative documents.

King Henry eventually heard of Lady Mortimer's action and the possible outcome that affected the succession to the throne, Mary being fourth in line. Peace of mind returned to Mary after the judgment of the Holy Father arrived: it was in favour of the Suffolk marriage. At least the duchess could put that trouble from her.

When the French war broke out in 1523, the new fleet was ready but the old fleet was lying neglected, so hurried measures had to be taken for the ships to be refurbished, new crews recruited, victuals and armaments put aboard. One of the heaviest tasks was the bringing aboard of the enormous sails from the riverbank sail-lofts.

New and old fleets were given the same orders (seeing that almost all the real fighting was being done in Italy). They had to supply the Calais garrison, keep the Channel open from end to end and, of course, destroy any French ships they could find.

The newer and slightly larger "Great Harry" was now the flagship carrying the flag of Admiral Sir Thomas Howard, the disciplinarian, who some years before had brought some order back to the navy. He had transferred from the *MARY ROSE*. Mary's ship now had to make do with a Vice-Admiral, Sir William Fitzwilliam.

This extremely large fleet swept the Channel as ordered. Several minor actions took place but no great sea battle was fought. It could be said that these skirmishes were useful, although little damage was done to the enemy.

In Italy the fighting was fierce, the Emperor eventually gaining the victory in the course of which he took prisoner King Francis I. The French Regent, Louise, wisely made an immediate peace with King Henry. One clause in the treaty (which gave Mary immense satisfaction) obliged France to pay the arrears of her dowry money and to make regular payments in the future. It solved immediate financial problems but it had little effect in the long term for the Queen/Duchess was incorrigible.

Once again warships were not needed and, following the custom of no war, no navy, the fleet made its way up the Thames to be laid up. Once more the ships were emptied of stores and armaments, sails stored ashore, crews paid off, only a handful of maintenance men left on board.

Royalty and courtiers in Greenwich Palace and the good people of the City of London for the whole of the next decade would have a melancholy view of the river crowded with lifeless and motionless great ships in slow decay.

In 1525, Duchess Mary went to London to be present with Brandon when the earldom of Lincoln was conferred on their only son Henry, aged nine. It was a proud moment for these parents: proof that the king still had great affection for his sister Mary.

There was one small fly in the ointment on that happy day. Henry decided to include in the investiture his much loved illegitimate son, Henry Fitzroy aged six, who was created Earl of Nottingham. Fitzroy was a charming little boy and the king was very fond of him.

With cessation of the French war, the French Regent, Louise of Savoy, began sending Mary the back payments of her French revenue and this was very welcome. Mary was glad also to be able to correspond once more with her friends in Paris - particularly with Jane Popincourt, the mistress of the Duc de Longueville, who sent her details of the latest fashions and samples of ladies' dress materials.

The Duchess of Suffolk was at court again in 1526 to attend at Greenwich the banquet given by the king in honour of the French ambassadors who had come to England on a special mission of friendship. Queen Claude had died and Francis I was looking for a bride. Accordingly, he made overtures to England for the hand of the ten-year-old Princess Mary of England, daughter of King Henry and Queen Katherine. The little lady had already been engaged once to Francis' son the Dauphin but the arrangement had been cancelled in favour of the Emperor Charles V. That second engagement had collapsed, and the princess was offered again a French husband but this time the Dauphin's father instead of the Dauphin.

Henry had ordered an enormous open-air banquet for the occasion to impress the French. It took place on the river bank with the anchored fleet in full view. The seating arrangements at the High Table caused raised eyebrows among both courtiers and the French delegation. Totally contrary to royal custom, the Duchess Mary was given precedence over the little Princess Mary. Was it a mistake? Did it mean something sinister in court language? Eventually the whole country would know. After the banquet, Henry went on a royal progress through Kent, during which he stayed at the small but very pretty moated Hever Castle the home of Sir Thomas Boleyn.

The following year saw a return of the French mission when the small princess showed off all her accomplishments - musical, linguistic and solo dancing. These impressed the Frenchmen but they reported to Paris that her body was extremely thin and that consummation should not be thought of for at least four years. Duchess Mary was again at the centre of the entertaining. Queen Katherine is not mentioned as being present, so presumably the king had deliberately kept her in the background, unless illness was the reason.

The year 1527 saw the most severe outbreak of the highly infectious "sweating sickness". Nobody knew how to treat the disease. Everyone was frightened when it appeared in a community - mostly in large towns. The only precaution that could be taken was to fly to the country and as far away as possible. It killed quickly - sometimes even in only one day. The death rate was extremely high and victims came from all classes of society. A great number of preposterous quack remedies were advocated but did no good, except perhaps to give some false comfort to the sufferers.

The eleven-year-old Earl of Lincoln, Mary's only son and apple of her eye, died of that malady. She was utterly desolated even though the death of a child was a familiar event in all families. The duchess received little support from her husband, for he spent almost all his time at court. The gradual deterioration of her health became accelerated, and although she struggled to London when royal duty called, she was in fact a broken woman, gradually losing her grasp on life.

Quite unexpectedly, at this time the Duke of Suffolk saw enormous increases in his fortune. Money and land seemed to come from every direction. The Emperor Charles V gave him a very big pension which was thought to be some kind of bribe for services rendered or to be rendered. Henry appointed his favourite to a number of salaried posts of which duties were minimal. When the Duke of Buckingham was attainted and his estates forfeit, Brandon somehow managed to acquire those manors that lay within the county of Suffolk - a very large acreage. Thus, his longstanding burden of debt began to be eased.

Chapter Eight

Queens and female nobility had always to accept as inevitable the infidelity of their husbands. Mary accepted this failing on the part of her duke and understood that he should provide for the fruit of illicit unions when this did not trespass on her own family life or humiliate her publicly. Her love for Brandon never faltered because of his adulteries. Queen Katherine also chose not to notice the king's long-standing liaisons with Elizabeth Blount and with Mary Boleyn as well as several more transitory attachments. Henry had been particularly fond of his son by Elizabeth Blount - he created him Duke of Richmond.

So it was that Katherine was not unduly put out when she learned of Henry's attraction to Anne Boleyn, one of her Maids of Honour. The queen became somewhat alarmed when she heard gossip that Anne had declined to be seduced. She conceded that the girl was pretty but she was far from being a beauty and was even slightly deformed in the neck and hand (very small deformities were considered as unwholesome in those times). Her husband's obsession with Anne she considered a mystery of ill-omen: something she failed to understand. Then slowly it began to dawn on her that the obsession with the Maid of Honour was linked to his other fierce obsession to beget a male heir.

Katherine's purgatory was about to begin, for her husband now began to avoid her. She was frequently ill and was visibly ageing. Soon the whole court knew what the queen knew. Her intimate friend and sister-in-law, the Queen/Duchess, heard the gossip and instantly her heart went out to the troubled wife who appreciated her message of sympathy. Quickly that whispering gallery, the court, passed on the news that Mary disapproved of her brother's actions. With a display of Tudor temper, the king made known his displeasure at her gesture.

Suffolk, the perfect court sycophant, continued to side with the king whatever he did or said. He rushed to reassure Henry of his support, to disparage Katherine and praise Anne. The duke was highly annoyed with his wife, thinking that her sympathy with Katherine would react to his disadvantage.

The domestic discord between king and queen was now beginning to be duplicated between the Suffolks. There was anger and coldness on his part and on hers stubbornness and grief. This did not lessen her love for her husband, which she felt until her death.

Mary's health declined while in the country and she stayed on at Westhorpe Manor. Charles remained at court, busily supporting every move the king made. Absence from court was the only way in which the Queen/Duchess could make her disapproval public. Mary had been an anointed queen herself and could not ignore her brother's cruelty towards his wife in pushing her aside for an adventuress. On the other hand, Suffolk was beholden to the king for everything he had. He had much of the parvenu in him and he was not going to ruin his position by retiring to the country to protest over something about which he had no scruples at all.

Soon, Henry let it be known that his conscience was troubled because he had committed the sin of marrying his brother's widow which made his marriage to Katherine null and void. He hinted that because of that sin his queen had not been able to give birth to a male heir.

Henry, through Wolsey, appealed to Queen Katherine to please him by taking the veil in a convent and taking, with his consent, religious vows. The queen would have none of it and told Wolsey this in no uncertain terms. The king then appealed to the Holy Father to make a decision to give his royal conscience some peace. Privately he said that Katherine was not at all well and her death might solve the problem. As it happened, Anne Boleyn caught the "sweating sickness" and was extremely ill, but she slowly recovered thus putting everything back to square one.

News came that Pope Clement VII was sending a legate, Cardinal Campeggio, to England to set up an enquiry. In 1529, the legate arrived in England and set up court at Blackfriars in London. The queen behaved throughout this enquiry with great dignity, and almost the whole country was on her side. The Londoners always shouted abuse at "Nan Bullen" when she appeared in public. The Suffolks were both in London for the hearing, but Mary could not bring herself to be present. Charles, however, eagerly presented himself as a witness when the Cardinal summoned to Blackfriars those who had evidence to give - including the king and the queen. Suffolk was willing to testify that on the morning after the wedding he met the Prince of Wales who said to him, "This night I have been to Spain," which he understood to mean that intercourse had taken place.

At the opening session, the king did not appear, but Katherine attended. She immediately announced that the Papal Legate was prejudiced against her, and she therefore appealed to Rome. She gave a low curtsey to the court and then left immediately. The Cardinal thought it impossible to proceed without the two chief witnesses, and accordingly requested both Henry and Katherine to appear personally at the next sitting in June. They both obeyed.

The king began by speaking a great tribute to his queen saying that she had been a wonderful wife and he was very unwilling to separate from her, but his conscience was worried about the illegality of marrying his brother's widow. The usher then called, "Katherine, Queen of England, come into court." At once Katherine rose to hear His Eminence say that her appeal to Rome had been denied. This statement she ignored and, crossing herself, accompanied by her ladies she walked right round the court. Stopping before the king she knelt down and spoke with a heavy Spanish accent for the whole court to hear:

> Sir, I beseech you, for all the loves there have been between us and for the love of God let me have some right and justice. Give me some pity and compassion for I am a poor stranger born out of your dominions. I have no unprejudiced counsellor and I fly to you as head of justice within your realm. Alas, wherein have I offended you? I take God and the whole world to witness that I have been to you a true humble and obedient wife, ever conformable to your will and your pleasure. I have been pleased and contented with all things wherein you found delight or dalliance. I loved all those you loved only for your sake whether they were my friends or enemies. These twenty years have I been your true wife and by me you have had several children although it has pleased God to call them out of the world which had been no fault of mine. I put it to your conscience whether I came not to you as a virgin. If you have since found any dishonour in my conduct then I am content to depart although to my great shame and disparagement but if none there are, then I beg you to let me remain in my proper state. The king your father was

91

accounted in his day as a second Solomon for wisdom and my father Ferdinand was esteemed one of the wisest kings that had ever reigned in Spain. They also had many learned counsellors who thought our marriage good and lawful. Therefore I marvel to hear what new inventions are brought up against me. Your subjects in this court dare not be impartial counsellors for they are frightened to disobey you. Therefore most humbly do I require you, in the way of charity and for the love of God, who is the just judge of all, to spare me the sentence of this. If you will not extend to me this favour your pleasure is fulfilled and to God do I commit my cause.[16]

Katherine then rose up, the tears streaming down her face. She made a low curtsey to the king and walked out of the court, ignoring the cry of the usher "Katherine, Queen of England, come again into court."

Eventually, Cardinal Campeggio, in agreement with Wolsey, adjourned the court, naming a date in October for the next hearing. Anne Boleyn was furious at this news and exerted all her influence with the king to have him dismissed and disgraced. In this she was supported by the Duke of Suffolk who always had Henry's ear.

While Wolsey was announcing the postponement, Brandon's patience gave out and he jumped to his feet livid with rage shouting: "By the Mass, it was never merry in England while we had cardinals among us." Very quietly Wolsey answered: "Sir, of all men within this realm you have least cause to dispraise cardinals for if I, poor cardinal, had not been, you should have at this present time no head upon your shoulders and no tongue wherewith you might make any such brag. You know best what friendship I showed you."[17] There was no answer from a highly embarrassed duke.

As for the two queens, neither of them liked Wolsey, but when they heard of the adjournment they knew that Henry's wrath would fall on him and that his fate was sealed. Both sincerely pitied him. To save his neck, the cardinal gave to the king everything that he had - two palaces, great estates, plate and jewels which would have been confiscated anyway - and resigned all his high positions in the state. His town residence, York House, the king renamed Whitehall, which became a popular royal palace as an alternative to Westminster. Kings had for some time abandoned the Tower as a residence.

It was Brandon who organised Wolsey's complete disgrace and banishment to York. Summoned back to London to answer serious charges, the cardinal died in a monastery on the way, which prevented his certain execution in the Tower for refusing to rubber-stamp his master's expressed desires.

That Christmas (1529), Queen Katherine presided over the court festivities, revellers being amazed at seeing the king with her again. Charles and Mary Brandon followed suit and they too enjoyed the return of the good old times. Christmas was always a wonderful time of magnificent religious services and perfect Gregorian chanting by choirs of monks, followed by jollifications. Then, as now, it was a time for healing family wounds. Disputes were forgotten and all were happy together. With the feast of the Three Kings (Epiphany) Mary returned to the country and stayed there in peace until the summer. Her husband remained at court. The king's "great matter" remained, and discord returned to the court to an even greater extent: all were frightened to think of what might happen next.

The Queen/Duchess became more and more unhappy about the situation. She was shocked at the growing power of Anne Boleyn, who had now been created "Marquess" of Pembroke, and maintained her own household in the manner of a queen. People who disagreed with the king and were sorry for Katherine were punished (two of her ladies were sent to the Tower), and there was every indication that many (including clergy) would soon have their heads separated from their shoulders.

All the protest Mary could make was to stay away from court. She passed the time by travelling from one house to another, from one monastery or convent to another. One of her interests was the raising of the standard of living of peasants who were scratching a meagre existence from the poor East Anglian soil, and with this end in view, she introduced hempen cloth and a new kind of Suffolk cheese. This was a very unusual activity for a Tudor princess. Quite unusual also was the simple and very happy pastime of playing games with her children and enjoying with them in the evenings music and dancing. She took the trouble to teach them herself these accomplishments.

Brandon was sent with Lord Rochford (Anne Boleyn's brother) to Italy on a mission to the Pope. It was a quick affair, for Suffolk hated being away from the king. He was always afraid that he might lose his position as favourite if he absented himself for too long. It had not gone unnoticed that his wife was violently opposed to the repudiation of Katherine and had begun to make her views known loudly. It was a reckless thing to do at that time, but the queen continued to be very popular.

In London, citizens chanted "King's Whore," when Anne processed through the streets heavily guarded.

Over the next few years, Henry broke all contact with Rome, establishing himself as Head of the Church of England. He dissolved all the religious houses and all shrines - some of the estates he seized himself, sold some at knock down prices, for too much land came on to the market at one time, and gave the rest away to his favourites.

Katherine was put under house arrest and her household reduced to a minimum. She was left without money. Lord Mountjoy was the king's messenger sent to inform the queen that her title was now Dowager Princess of Wales and that her daughter, Mary, was now illegitimate. Katherine refused to accept the order for her attendants to address her by this new title and her ladies were then threatened with punishment. Mountjoy (her former page) became so abusive and insulting that the queen brought the audience to an end by retiring into another room.

Almost everyone in England now took sides as the controversy grew. Most women sided with Katherine and openly said so. In many cases, married women had contrary views to their husbands, just as the duke and duchess of Suffolk did. The secular clergy, monks and nuns were all against the divorce. A majority of the nobles and nearly all the courtiers supported Henry and urged separation from Katherine and Rome.

The king told the queen to spend Christmas with him at Greenwich in 1530 when he showed much affection for her and for his infant daughter, Mary, who was a little afraid of her father. During the festivities, he asked Katherine to withdraw her appeal to Rome which she said she was unable to do. At once Henry left for the palace of Whitehall and sulked. At Whitsuntide the following year, he again approached the queen to persuade her to cancel her appeal to the Pope, and when she again had to say she regretted her inability to do so, King Henry went wild with rage.

A little later (June 1531), both king and queen were at Windsor, and he evidently came to a sudden decision at the prompting of Anne, for he left the castle abruptly, sending a message to the queen to depart from her apartments there before he returned. At once she retired to one of her manors in Hertfordshire. She never again saw her husband or her daughter (who had already been taken from her). As she went away from Windsor she said, "Go where I may, I am his wife and for him will I pray."

Every messenger from court seemed to bring the Duchess Mary bad news of her friends, but in her isolated countryside she was able to occupy herself and so forget the events she so much deplored.

In the spring of 1532, the duchess came to court for a short time at the request of the duke. When in conversation with the Venetian Ambassador, she expressed herself about Anne Boleyn with such violence and abuse that her remarks were repeated to the king who flew into such a rage, even threatening prison, that she immediately escaped to her country retreat to avoid punishment. Thoroughly frightened, she remained quietly at Westhorpe Hall for the rest of the year.

Henry made an alliance with Francis I in 1532, and arranged for a conference in France which was to be something like the Field of the Cloth of Gold but on a much more modest scale. Mary was commanded to attend but as Anne was going with him she refused. This infuriated both the king and Suffolk, and Mary expected to be arrested. But nothing happened, probably because the French also delivered a similar snub: the French Queen and Marguerite de Valois declined the invitation having no wish to meet the upstart Anne. Duke Charles was obliged to travel to Calais alone, as his absence would have angered the king, but he was greatly vexed with his wife and told her so in several enraged letters. This incident led to further coldness and a cessation of correspondence for a time.

Events moved rapidly in that year. The Archbishop of Canterbury died and the "King's man," Cranmer, was appointed to the vacancy. The House of Commons declared in favour of Katherine and asked Henry to take her back as his wife. The king set up a court in Dunstable which declared against the queen and ruled that both parties could re-marry. In January, very early in the morning and in the greatest secrecy, and by a royal chaplain summoned at the last minute, Henry and Anne were married. Anne was pregnant - hence the hurry. She immediately went into retirement until it was pointed out to the king that a public marriage was essential to safeguard the legitimacy of Anne's child, the long awaited heir to the throne. So in April 1533, the couple went through a second marriage ceremony with all the officers of the state attending. By now Anne had been given her own royal household and was addressed as Queen.

That spring, the Queen/Duchess found that her general health was deteriorating. She was not satisfied with the skill of the local country doctors who attended her and decided to ask

95

her brother for permission to come to London and consult the royal physicians:

My most dearest and best beloved brother, I humbly recommend me to your grace. Sir, so it is that I have been very sick and ill at ease for the which I was fain to send for Master Peter the Fesysyon to help me with the disease that I have. If I tarry here I am sure I shall never asperge the sickness that I have. Wherefore, Sir, I would be the gladder to come thither because I would be glad to see your grace the which I do long for to do. The sight of your grace is the greatest comfort to me that may be possible. I pray God to send your heart's desire and the sight of you. By your loving sister, Mary the French Queen.[18]

The required permission was given and Mary came up to London looking like the invalid she was.

By now Mary had settled both her stepdaughters. Lady Anne Brandon was now Lady Powis and Lady Mary Brandon was engaged to Lord Monteagle.

She brought with her her two daughters for whom she had found husbands. In passing, it could be mentioned as a medical curiosity that the Queen/Duchess was below average height and that both her daughters were even shorter. Their four daughters were shorter still, and indeed, two of them could truthfully be described as dwarfs. One of them, Lady Mary Grey, the smallest of all, was really minute, and she married a giant of over two metres in height who was the gate keeper of a royal palace. There was no issue of that marriage.

The wedding of Lady Frances Brandon to the Marquess of Dorset, and the engagement ceremony of Lady Eleanor Brandon to Lord Henry Clifford (later Earl of Cumberland), took place in May in the presence of their uncle King Henry. No mention is made of Anne Boleyn so presumably Henry came without her.

Mary had no benefit from the doctors she consulted, and decided to return to Westhorpe Manor. Her daughter Eleanor travelled with her, but the duke, with Dorset and Clifford, was obliged to remain in London as they had to carry out duties at the coming coronation of Queen Anne, which had been arranged for the end of the month. Both Dorset and Clifford were now Knights of the Bath. Suffolk had been appointed Anne's Lord High Steward for the occasion.

After passing the night at the Tower, which was traditional before a coronation, Anne travelled in a horse litter covered with cloth of gold, escorted by the duke and Dorset riding white horses on either side. Fountains ran with wine in the City and the new queen was greeted with shouts of approval by the fickle citizens. She was delighted with her reception and proudly acknowledged the ovation. The archbishops of Canterbury and York, nobility, ambassadors, Yeomen of the Guard, Lord Mayor and civil dignitaries were all in the procession. Her dress was of silver tissue under a cloak of velvet lined with ermine. Her dark hair was worn loose and on her head she had a coronet of large rubies.

At the Abbey she was crowned with the ancient St Edward's Crown and was handed the sceptre by Mary's son-in-law Dorset. Suffolk and Dorset carried out their duties at the banquet later when the ceremony of the washing of the Queen's hands was performed. As royalty, she was now served "on the knee."

Poor Anne. She had struggled so hard to reach a crown, and now she had achieved her ambition; the crowd paid her homage and the king was her servant. The fingers that put the wedding ring on her finger within three years would sign her death certificate, and her husband would wait impatiently for the boom of the cannon which told him her head had rolled from her shoulders.

At the time of the coronation, Mary was seriously ill at Westhorpe, otherwise she would never have been excused attendance for she had, as the king's sister, traditional duties on such an occasion. Her two daughters, Frances and Eleanor, were with her. Suffolk, Dorset and Clifford were all at court.

In the evening of 25th June 1533, Mary Princess, sometime queen, later duchess, died quietly in the presence of her daughters.

The body of the Queen/Duchess was embalmed and lay in state in the chapel of Westhorpe Hall for three weeks in order that there was adequate time for the funeral to be organised. Charles Suffolk came from London for a day or two but then returned to the capital to press for his wife's French revenues to continue to be paid. Masses were said every day in the chapel, and Frances and Eleanor spent most of the time by their mother's corpse praying for the repose of her soul. Requiem Masses were said daily in Westminster Abbey and St Paul's Cathedral: this was to enable courtiers and her friends to pay their last respects.

Henry did not offer a state funeral with burial in a royal tomb in one of the royal churches, and it was gossip that the reason for that was Anne's vindictiveness and the king's anger

97

at Mary's support for Katherine. It was the custom for a king not to go into the country for a funeral, so there was an excuse for Henry, who had no wish to attend. As far as is known, he did not attend one of the London Masses either. The dead duchess was an anointed queen of France and so an official delegation had to come from Paris to represent King Francis. Nobody represented King Henry.

On 20th July, the funeral cortege left her favourite home. Official and personal mourners had arrived from London and Paris, as well as monks and nuns from the communities she had helped. According to royal custom, an effigy of the dead queen in full regalia was carried in the long procession. The corpse was enclosed in a lead coffin placed inside a wooden casket, which was covered by a blue velvet pall. The gentlemen of the household carried the coffin to the hearse. Garter King-at-Arms led the procession, followed by several heralds and poursuivants in mediaeval uniforms. The passing bell tolled continuously from churches throughout East Anglia and from some in London.

The hearse itself was drawn by six heavy black horses, covered with black velvet embroidered with designs incorporating the Tudor Rose and the French Lily. Lady Frances and Lady Eleanor rode black horses and were escorted by the Marquess of Dorset and Lord Henry Clifford. They were followed by Gentlemen of the Household, Maids of Honour, Nobility, local secular clergy, personal servants, local officials, peasants from neighbouring villages. By the roadside at intervals stood little knots of elderly people holding candles paying a tribute to the great lady whose alms had helped them.

It took a whole day for the cortege to wind through the rough road and reach the Abbey of St Edmund. The coffin was taken before the High Altar for the monks to keep vigil during the night. The pall, carrying the queen's device and her motto "La volonté de Dieu me suffit" was on the casket. Before the mourners dispersed for the night, the French poursuivant cried out in a loud voice the customary invitation "Pray for the Soul of the Right High and Excellent Princess and Right Christian Queen Mary, late French Queen - and for all Christian Souls."

After the third Mass the following day, the De Profundis was said as the coffin was lowered into the vault and then the Gentlemen of the Household broke their wands of Office and threw the pieces into the grave amid general lamentation.

The funeral feast provided excellent food for the tired mourners and for the general public meat and drinks of beer were distributed at various centres in the town for all comers.

The unfortunate poor of the area were each given a dole of fourpence. The French Queen was long remembered in East Anglia. Nobody replaced her. In French history books, she is remembered for her surpassing loveliness, gentleness of character and for her short stay in France as consort.

The Princess Mary Tudor was probably the most beautiful lady of the century. Even in death she kept her good looks and her mass of fine long fair hair. Every court in Europe knew of her, and ambassadors in England were asked to pass an opinion on the famous beauty. Perhaps better than her looks was her lovely welcoming smile (an asset for royalty) and she was graceful of movement - a real gift when clothed in the stiff dresses of the period. She was loved and indulged by her father, her brother and by her royal husband in turn.

Alone of the Tudor princesses, by expert manoeuvring she married for passionate love and never regretted it, even though Suffolk was casually unfaithful and did not return her love with equal intensity. During their time together (before Anne Boleyn brought a coldness between them), they had hilarious country holidays and endless fun and laughter.

As a small child, her brother Arthur was Prince of Wales. It was another Prince of Wales, Charles, who was present when her ship was raised from the mud. Mary and both Princes of Wales are descended from Henry VII.

Is the beauty of the Princess a myth? Has her beauty been exaggerated? Has due allowance been made for the custom of the period to see all female royalty as lovely and charming?

Existing portraits do not portray anything exceptional about her looks - perhaps the artist was not skilful - so we must rely on the judgment and written word of contemporary men and women. Those who saw her grew lyrical in their praises. Courtiers, ambassadors, relatives, all thought her the loveliest of creatures and mentioned graceful movement and her sweet smile. These writings are plentiful in France but mention of this beauty exists in several countries in records and libraries. Today we can be certain that stories about her appearance are fact and not fiction.

Was her character as good as her looks? It is not being naive to answer a loud "Yes". She followed the custom of her century by accepting the system of political marriage for her first union but, relying on her brother's word, refused a second, using her head to support strong reasons of the heart. She had a passion for jewelry but gave away a mountain of it for love. Her husband was a truly repulsive figure, unfit for a young bride, but she carefully avoided giving him the impression of disgust, and showed him every respect because

99

he was so wonderfully kind to her.

At the end of her life, she refused to condone injustice to a queen who had shown her affection all her life. It would have been easy for her to join her ambitious husband and shun the ageing, ill and insulted queen to welcome her successor. She could have approved her brother's evil actions but she did not.

She was charity itself to countless poor. She loved her religion, although she did not share Katherine's urge to multiply her mortifications.

Was she a good mother? Yes. Unlike almost every royal mother of the time she enjoyed her children's company, played and romped with them in her country home which she and they truly loved.

What was the reason for the rift between brother and sister when they had been so affectionate since early childhood? Did Mary feel that the king was undermining Holy Religion? It possibly did not cross her mind except when seizure of church land and the dissolution of religious houses was suggested - she was very fond of staying as a guest in monasteries and convents. She had long known that kings often tried to bend religious laws to suit their own convenience.

Was it a deep dislike of the personality of Anne Boleyn? Probably, yes. She profoundly regretted seeing a brother in his forties make such a weak fool of himself, instead of treating the woman as just another mistress, which was thought to be the proper behaviour for a monarch. Royalty was always allowed greater leniency for human frailty than other men.

Was it a fierce loyalty to Katherine? Yes. There was no doubt that she wished to visit Katherine, but it was not permitted. In spite of a fear of making matters worse, she did try to broach the subject with the king, who refused to discuss it. She suffered greatly for the queen's suffering. Katherine knew of this and was grateful.

What were the reasons for the rift with her husband: a rift so deep that married relations between them ceased and, from time to time, also communications? Was it Charles' extramarital relations? No, she was well used to these and accepted them. Was it Charles' attitude of agreeing with everything the king did in order to retain his position as favourite at all costs? Yes, but Mary did not find this extraordinary, as Suffolk had done just that all his life. Was it that she found it inexcusable for him to treat an anointed queen with such cruelty and disrespect? Yes, Mary found it incomprehensible.

Did she still love Charles? Yes. Without any doubt she longed for him to return to the country and live away from that dreadful court and find some peace and tranquillity with her. But that was not in the duke's nature, even if there had been no Anne Boleyn.

Nobody at that time, least of all those near the throne, realised that the shadow of Anne Boleyn would lie across many people until the beginning of the following century. History is full of "ifs" and "buts" and idle unprofitable speculation - the smallest accidents or incidents can change even the life of a nation. The courtship and marriage of Anne affected the very succession to the English throne and for a half-century caused endless trouble and unrest and rivers of blood. Henry altered by will the succession (which he had no right to do), and included children by various wives. That brought into question the legitimacy of his issue. The word "bastard" was hurled against the three following sovereigns with great freedom.

This shadow fell on all Mary's grandchildren, who were believed to nourish a secret ambition to the throne before the (rightful) Scottish claimants the descendants through Henry VIII's eldest sister, Queen Margaret of Scotland.

Because of the confusion caused by the king's will, Lady Jane Grey was decapitated at the age of fifteen, Lady Katherine Grey was a prisoner in the Tower for most of her life in the hope that she would die childless, Lady Mary Grey was under strict house arrest for thirteen years with the same object. The last of the grandchildren, Lady Margaret Clifford, was arrested on a trumped up charge and remained for sixteen years under house restriction. Fortunately the young Earl of Lincoln died before worse happened to him.

❀ ❀ ❀

What was the relationship between Mary and the *MARY ROSE*? Suffolk (because of his official position at court) and the Queen/Duchess saw a great deal of the ship from the windows of Greenwich Palace and Suffolk House and also on her frequent journeys up and down the Thames by barge. But for most of the long periods when the fleet was in the river the *MARY ROSE* was stripped and without sails and therefore not a happy sight. The king with the duke inspected the fleet occasionally and went aboard the big ships which included the *MARY ROSE* and the *HENRY GRACE A DIEU*. The visit of Katherine and Mary to the *VIRGIN QUEEN* for a banquet is fully documented, and it seems certain that both dined several times on other ships, including the *MARY ROSE*. Full banqueting facilities were available on these large warships and the court took advantage of this popular thing to do especially on a beautiful summer evening.

Chapter 9

Charles Suffolk grew continually more discourteous to Queen Katherine when she had fallen from favour and was friendless. This was particularly mean, for she had shown him nothing but genuine friendship. When the queen was downgraded to Dowager Princess of Wales, her supply of money was cut off and her household reduced to almost nothing. From time to time, Henry sent messengers offering bribes to accept the new title but she refused to do so, insisting that she was the king's wife and her daughter, Mary, his legitimate daughter. She never moved from that position.

Charles was the messenger sent by Henry to break up the queen's extremely small household when she was under house arrest at Buckden. He wished to reduce the number of attendants even further and keep only those who would take the oath "I swear to bear faith, troth and obedience only to the King's Grace and to the heirs of his body by his most dear and entirely beloved lawful wife Queen Anne."[19] It was the duke who arranged her forced and final journey to Kimbolton Castle where she died. He used such rough and insulting words to her that she could not bear to hear more and rose from her chair to leave the room in tears. From then on, she had no money at all, and could not pay her ladies, which was a great grief to her. Her very agèd confessor was taken to the Tower, tortured and eventually burnt to death. From then on Katherine learned of clerical and lay friends being executed for refusing to recognise her divorce.

Six weeks after the death of the Duchess Mary, Brandon married again - doubtless for financial reasons - the wealthy

Lady Katherine Willoughby who was fourteen at the time. She gave him two sons who died when very young, within a day or two of each other and in the same bed.

Katherine of Aragon died in 1536, sad and lonely in her unhealthy castle. To the last, she refused to revile Anne for the sake of Christian charity telling an attendant to pray for Lady Anne and pity her. Within four months Anne had died a frightful death by the axe on Tower Hill. When the king learned of Katherine's death he wept and re-read her pathetic letters. He then seized what little property she had left in her prison.

After ten years of naval peace and with most of the fleet lying in the river, in 1536 a complete refit was ordered. It was probably carried out in the Thames where facilities were available. Fortunately the work was done thoroughly and the ships appeared as new with completely fresh fittings and armaments. It was difficult to believe that some of the ships were twenty-five years old and had seen a number of fierce actions.

In 1538, the dissolution of the monasteries was in full swing and the wreckers arrived at the huge abbey of St Edmund in the county of Suffolk.

After spending much time with pickaxes, it was found that little progress was being made so it was decided to use explosives to shatter the fabric. Sometimes when monastery buildings were destroyed the tombs were desecrated and the bodies thrown out into the fields after it was certain that no jewelry was buried with the corpses. But before the St Edmund's abbey monks were expelled, they wished to find a secure place for the remains of their benefactress the French Queen, and so they moved her wooden coffin to the local Parish Church and placed it under a large stone which most likely came from the High Altar of their abbey and which the Fathers wished secretly to preserve.

In the general destruction her monument over the abbey

103

tomb disappeared. But the monks, before leaving the area, cut the name MARY QUENE on the slab in parish church of St Mary.

King Henry certainly knew of the demolition of the abbey but he showed no interest in caring for his sister's grave or magnificent funeral monument in alabaster which he himself had paid for in part.

In the year 1544, England attacked Boulogne, the Duke of Suffolk being in command. He was successful and ordered the desecration of the church of Notre Dame in that town. He confiscated the ancient statue of Our Lady of Boulogne, packed it in a crate and sent it to King Henry who placed it in his bedroom. It was a most strange action on Henry's part, for over the past few years he had organised the wholesale destruction of statues at shrines and in churches all over England by burning them publicly.

The king became nervous about 1544 that his chief naval port was inadequately protected and feared that a strong French raid might mean the wholesale destruction of ships. He therefore engaged a German military engineer to design and construct a series of low profile forts or castles round Spithead and the Solent, arming these with the heaviest cannon. Southsea Castle was built at that time. Once again the seesaw of political alliances changed and Henry became the ally of the Emperor Charles V, commencing a struggle against his former friend Francis I of France. The arrangement was that English troops would attack and seize Boulogne and then march on Paris.

Not much later the Emperor made a peace treaty behind Henry's back and so England was left to fight King Francis alone. It was a very serious situation.

In 1545, Francis saw a golden opportunity to defeat the English decisively. He sent a large army to retake Boulogne, at the same time assembling a huge fleet under the command of Claude d'Annebault, Baron de Retz, which included the twenty-five galleons of the Baron de la Garde. The immediate aim was to destroy the English navy and their base at Portsmouth. The secondary objective was to take Calais and totally expel the English from the land of France. Presumably if these aims were attained, a French army would land on the south coast for a full scale invasion.

The fight started badly for the French. Francis had given a banquet on board the flagship *CARRAQUON* and then gone on shore with the court to climb the cliffs and watch the armada put to sea. It is thought that careless (or drunk) cooks caused a fire which ran through the whole ship so quickly that the crew were helpless - it became just one sheet of flame. Worse still, the fire caused the cannon to fire and the gun powder to explode which spread the damage and sank seveal other ships. Many sailors and soldiers were either burnt or drowned.

The king and the royal party watching on the cliffs were shocked and helpless. Eventually the king ordered the admiral to take command in another flagship *LA MAISTRESSE* but she too became a temporary casualty by running aground although with much effort by towing she was refloated undamaged. The fleet then got under way for England. The French had some galleys in their fleet and these were more easily manoeuvred than the English warships.

Henry VIII was now in Portsmouth reviewing and inspecting the fleet and visiting the dockyard. He gave a magnificent banquet on the *HENRI GRACE A DIEU* (Great Harry) for the Lord Admiral of England, Sir John Dudley, Viscount Lisle. Sir George Carew, Vice-Admiral was now in command of the *MARY ROSE* and was also a guest. After the banquet on the Great Harry everything was cleared for action. The French had further bad luck at this time, for it was discovered that *LA MAISTRESSE* had suffered severe damage after being towed from the sandbank and she had to be beached on the Isle of Wight. The French admiral had to carry his flag on yet a third ship.

When the look-out shouted that French ships were approaching, the king called for his barge and was taken to the shore just below Southsea Castle where he joined his court. They proposed to watch the battle. Lady Carew was one of the company by special invitation of King Henry. The Duke of Suffolk, who was in charge of the land force assembled to defeat any possible French invaders, was either with his men drawn up on Southsea Common or else on the castle ramparts with the king.

It was a most exciting ocasion, for rarely, if ever, had a monarch with his court watched a full scale naval battle at such close range. The rival forces were not evenly matched, for Francis had well over thirty thousand fighting men in over two hundred ships while Henry could boast only a quarter of the ships and less than half of the men. Although smaller, the English navy made a brave sight with sails billowing, flags flying and long pennants streaming in the breeze. Gunfire continued and it seemed to the watchers that the French were not prepared to attack but rather draw away the English ships from the protection of the shore batteries and then finish them off with superior gunfire further out at sea.

The *MARY ROSE* began to move across the waters of Spithead. On the way, another English ship passed her whose commander shouted to Sir George Carew to enquire whether all was well aboard, for he thought he detected a slight list. Sir George shouted back that all was in order except that he had a lot of disobedient knaves aboard. The handsome warship pushed by a breeze sailed close inshore right in front of Southsea Castle. The old lady looked an inspiring sight, the veteran of highly successful actions against the French. Lady Carew must have been apprehensive as perhaps all the other ladies in the royal party for assuredly they had never seen anything like it before. It was exciting but it could become highly dangerous. Unique it was and very dramatic.

Suddenly the large number of onlookers became vaguely aware that all was not well with the *MARY ROSE* which had just sailed before them going into action, and a feeling of uneasiness swept through the crowd on the castle ramparts. Then in a flash, the ship heeled over, and before the horrified gaze of king and court, the splendid warship sank, leaving only her masts with attached pennants protruding from the water. The cries of numbers of drowning men came across the water and nobody could help. Small rowing boats were quickly launched from the beach and were able to save a few who were clinging to the masts. The whole court was in despair. Henry hid his face in his hands moaning for "My gentlemen, my fine gentlemen." The ladies clung to each other and wept. Only about thirty men were saved out of more than five hundred. Lady Carew's husband was one of the drowned as was the ship's captain, Roger Grenville. The French saw what had happened and thought that she had been sunk by French gunfire.

The reason for the sinking is not known - yet. There have been suggestions that a squall struck the ship and that the gun port lids being raised water poured in. Even naval experts cannot be definite.

Instead of pressing on with their action, the French unexpectedly withdrew. They landed on the Isle of Wight, burnt and looted a number of villages, then returned to their ships.

The French fleet decided to make one of the usual raids on the English coast before returning to France. Accordingly, a raiding party was landed at Seaford. The raiders retired when a detachment of the Kent and Sussex militia (which defended that section of the coast) appeared on the scene.

After the first few hours of despair, efforts were made to salvage the *MARY ROSE* by dragging her into shallower waters. The Duke of Suffolk appointed salvage men for this task. Two ships, the *JESUS DE LUBECK* and the *SAMSON*, were secured on each side of the wreck perhaps to benefit from tidal lift but the attempt was a total failure. Diving equipment at the time was based on the bell principle and was quite primitive. It is not surprising that later on the duke called off the rescue.

In 1545, the same year that the *MARY ROSE* was wrecked, the Duke of Suffolk died at Guildford Castle in the presence of his two daughters and a grandchild, Lady Katherine Grey. In his will, he requested that he should be buried without any pomp in a village church in Lincolnshire but Henry VIII countermanded this and arranged for something much grander to honour his life-long intimate and brother-in-law. So there was a very opulent funeral at Windsor, similar to that of the Queen/Duchess in 1533, except that the signs of royalty were missing. The duke was buried in an important tomb just inside the entrance of St George's Chapel, Windsor. Requiem Masses were said there and at Westminster Abbey and St Paul's Cathedral. These were attended by the great of the nation, for he had been the unchallenged favourite of the king for nearly fifty years.

He left his property to his widow (his fifth wife) with reversion to his daughters Frances, Marchioness of Dorset and Eleanor, Countess of Cumberland. His widow married her very young secretary, Mr Bertie, who was an extreme Protestant. This so angered Mary I that the couple fled to Italy and Poland to return to England only after Mary's death.

About 1570, another attempt at salvage was made on the *MARY ROSE* wreck but again it seems to have been completely unsuccessful because diving techniques of the period were not sufficiently advanced.

In Bury, Suffolk, in 1781, it was decided to enlarge the parish church of St Mary. In the chancel, while this work was being done, a wooden coffin, much decayed, was discovered. Inside that casket a leaden coffin was seen and, on being exposed, the inscription "Marye, Quene of Ffrance 1533" noticed. Sir John Cullum, who was in charge of the project, happened to be present, and he took it upon himself to open the lead coffin which revealed a body in an almost perfect state of preservation.

The little group of spectators was amazed at the exquisite beauty of the woman who seemed to be sleeping. The long fine golden hair spread over the body like a cloak, reaching below her waist. The spectators, composed of building workers and townsfolk hurriedly summoned, awestruck at finding themselves in the presence of such loveliness, realised that they were looking at a French Queen. The flesh was still supple and had its natural colouring and many began to poke it with their fingers. Yes, it was true. Time had stood still for the Princess Mary.

Disgracefully, Sir John, like a vulture, bent down and snipped some of the beautiful hair from the corpse and immediately the crowd joined in, pushing each other in their eagerness to clip a lock as a souvenir. Within an hour, there was no hair left and the queen's beauty had been mutilated. Quick orders were given for immediate re-burial before further desecration was done.

Soon small locks of golden hair were being exposed for sale in shop windows and some even appeared as lots in auctions. Collectors paid highly for this royal relic, and among others the Duke of Buckingham and Sir Horace Walpole managed to secure specimens. Eventually, the stone slab (reputedly the altar stone of the demolished St Edmund's Abbey Church) was placed over the remains to prevent more sacrilege.

By the eighteen thirties, there had been some advances in technical equipment for underwater exploration although it was still rather crude compared with modern sophisticated apparatus. At that time, there were two men by the name of Dean who accepted a Government contract to discover and attempt salvage of Spithead wrecks. It is likely that they chose wrecks in shallow water and ships carrying valuables. They probably learned very quickly that Spithead is rather special. There are strong currents and visibility is extemely poor. On the bed are mudbanks which constantly move. From the *MARY ROSE*, the Deans were only able to recover some guns, pottery, wood and skulls.

Victorians were always greatly interested in death, manner of dying, graves, funeral monuments and the queen was no exception. After the death of the Prince Consort, this interest increased and approached morbidity. As the years passed, the obsession decreased but Victoria always retained a respect and reverence - even tenderness - for the dead.

When it came to her notice that the corpse of a royal personage had been desecrated, she had an instant sympathy with the defenceless remains, and had steps taken to ensure no further profanity occurred, by raising a monument at her own expense.

In this way she cared for the re-burial of the fifteen-year-old Princess Elizabeth who died in Carisbrooke Castle in 1650 after years of imprisonment, and had a marble statue erected showing the unfortunate daughter of Charles I just as she died - falling asleep with her head on the open Bible.

The queen in 1881 was distressed to learn that the tomb of the French Queen in Bury St Edmunds had been defaced and that further damage was possible. She at once ordered the tomb itself to be repaired and a marble slab placed with an inscription to identify the grave. A commemorative window was placed in the church.

Mr Alexander McKee, an amateur diver from Hayling Island near Portsmouth, began to explore the sea bed of Spithead in 1965. He had a special interest in discovering and identifying the great number of wrecks in the area and making a map of their locations: a difficult and painstaking task, even though diving equipment had improved and was very sophisticated.

The local swimmers and divers began to hear of Mr McKee's activities and joined him, his enthusiasm being infectious. Leisure time diving as a sport became almost a working schedule as the team collected more and more information about the location of Spithead wrecks - some known and documented and others a complete surprise. More young men were attracted to the group which began to concentrate on the *MARY ROSE* because it was such an interesting wreck, fully documented and most likely rich in artefacts. Eventually the ship was located and markers were placed. The first few artefacts were brought to the light of day.

As time passed, an experienced archaeologist, Dr Margaret Rule, who was then working on excavations at the Roman occupation palace of King Cogidubnus near Chichester, became fascinated by the story of the *MARY ROSE* and the efforts of local enthusiasts. She was naturally interested in the fate of the objects once on the surface and so brought the knowledge of an archaeologist to the venture. The preservation of articles brought suddenly into the air after several hundred years in sea water was a science in its infancy. Not sufficient was known about it, although a great deal had been learned by the Swedes who had brought the wreck of their ship *WASA* to the surface some time before. Dr Rule took lessons in diving and in due course the idea of raising the *MARY ROSE* in one piece was born.

It was rather a wild scheme because there was nowhere to put the ship once it had been raised. How could it be towed to land? How was the enormous cost to be raised? Would not all the timber disintegrate on breaking surface into air?

There was some good publicity and the idea caught the imagination of romantics and historians countrywide. Even children helped. Eventually the **Mary Rose Trust** was formed. The rich find of artefacts - thousands of them - contributed to the excitement, and by now every article recovered was cared for, identified and catalogued in a scientific manner. There was everything likely to be found on a great warship of the period: guns, bows, arrows, swords, buttons, buckles, jewelry, armour, coins, rope, anchors, compasses, kitchen utensils, cutlery, plates, cups, glasses, bottles, shoes, clothes, medical instruments.

The ship had sunk so quickly and in calm weather that in spite of currents the artefacts were found more or less where they were when they first reached the sea bed.

Now that more funds were available in the Trust, it became possible to put more equipment on site and to buy a base vessel and moor it. Then Earl Mountbatten of Burma visited the location and inspected some of the finds. He gave a great deal of assistance and lost no time in interesting HRH Charles, Prince of Wales, who was already an enthusiastic archaeologist and sea diver. Things then really began to move. A heavy steel "cradle" was designed and constructed, which could be used for raising the wreck and then a floating crane would, it was fondly hoped, lift the *MARY ROSE* and deposit her on a huge barge. It surprised nobody when the Prince decided he could not miss the thrill of seeing the ship slowly appear on the surface. He did more: he took an underwater look to inspect progress.

Crowds stood on the shore at Southsea; crane and barges were on site; television cameramen occupied vantage points. Some people stood on the ramparts of Southsea Castle exactly where the king and his courtiers stood in 1545. As the wreck finally broke surface in its steel cradle, sirens blew and there was a gun salute from the castle.

But in one terrible moment, just clear of the water, something went wrong. Cradle and cargo gave a frightening jerk to one side. Millions watching just held their breath: it just could not be true. One could not sit and see the *MARY ROSE* slide back again into the sea! Had it all been for nothing?

Eventually cradle with ship inside were stabilised, and were placed on the waiting barge to be towed back to Portsmouth Dockyard where *MARY ROSE* had been built.

Later she was put into dry dock to undergo study and conservation so that she can safely be put on display with thousands of salvaged artefacts and become a living history lesson.

To those of us who are romantics, the pleasure of the raising day was heightened by the présence of HRH Charles, Prince of Wales who is a descendant of the Queen Mary of France through her daughter Lady Frances Brandon and the great Seymour family: a name which constantly appears through the centuries of the English story.

Her Royal Highness Diana, Princess of Wales, is also a descendant of the "ffrenche Quene" through both of Mary's daughters and no less than five lines.

And the Tudor Princess, French Queen and Duchess of Suffolk, in her day known to all European courts and then almost forgotten to English history, has become well known again through the recovery of the *MARY ROSE* named for her as a compliment from a loving and admiring brother and as a tribute to her childhood beauty.

QUEEN AND DUKE

Eighth Henry ruling this land
   He had a sister fair,
That was the widow'd Queen of France,
   Enriched with virtues rare.
And being come to England's Court
   She oft beheld a knight,
Charles Brandon nam'd in whose fair eyes
   She chiefly took delight.

And noting in her princely mind
   His gallant sweet behaviour
She daily drew him by degrees
   Still more and more in favour.
Which he perceiving, courteous knight
   Found fitting time and place
And thus in amorous sort began
   His love-suit to her grace.

I am at love, fair Queen, said he
   Sweet, let your love incline,
That by your grace Charles Brandon may
   On earth be made divine.
If worthless I might worthy be
   To have so good a lot,
To please your highness in true love
   My fancy doubteth not.

Or if that gentry might convey
   So great a grace to me,
I can maintain the same by birth
   Being come of good degree.
If wealth you think be all my want
   Your Highness hath great store
And my supplement shall be love.
   What can you wish for more?

It hath been known when hearty love
    Did tie the true-love knot
Though now if gold and silver want
    The marriage proveth not.
The goodly queen hereat did blush
    But made a dumb reply
Which he imagined what she meant
    And kissed her reverently.

Brandon (quoth she) I greater am
    Than would I were for thee
But can as little master love
    As them of low degree.
My father was a king, and so
    A king my husband was.
My brother is the like and he
    Will say I do transgress.

But let him say what pleaseth him,
    His liking I'll forego
And chuse a love to please myself
    Though all the world say no.
If plowmen make their marriages
    As best contents their mind
Why should not princes of estate
    The like contentment find?

But tell me Brandon, am I not
    More forward than beseems?
Yet blame me not for love, I love
    Where best my fancy deems.
And long may live (quoth he) to love,
    Nor longer live may I
Than when I love your royal grace
    And then disgracèd die.

But if I do deserve your love
    My mind desires dispatch
For many are the eyes in court
    That on your beauty watch.
But am not I, sweet lady, now
    More forward than behoves?
Yet for my heart, forgive my tongue,
    That speaks for him that loves.

The queen and this grave gentleman
    Together both did wed
And after sought the king's goodwill
    And of their wishes sped.
For Brandon soon was made a duke
    And gracèd so in court
And who but he did flaunt it forth
    Amongst the noblest sort.

And so from princely Brandon's line
    And Mary did proceed
The noble race of Suffolk's house
    As after did succeed.
And whose high blood the lady Jane
    Lord Guildford Dudley's wife
Came by descent who, with her lord
    In London lost her life.

Unknown rhymist of the Sixteenth Century in
Suffolk Garland.

Princess Mary Tudor
1496 - 1533

m (1st) — King Louis 12th of France
1462 - 1515
No Issue — 1514

m (2nd) 1515 — Charles Brandon, Duke of Suffolk
1481 - 1545
Had Issue

Lady Frances Brandon
1517 - 1559
m 1533

Henry Grey,
2nd Marquess of Dorset
1517 - 1554
Beheaded

Lady Eleanor Brandon
1524 - 1547
m 1536

Henry Clifford
2nd Earl of Cumberland
1517 - 1570

Lady Margaret Clifford
1540 - 1596
Henry Stanley,
4th Earl of Derby
King of Man
1531 - 1593

Henry, Earl of Lincoln
1516 - 1527

Lady Jane Grey
1538 - 1553
Beheaded
m 1553

Lord Guildford
Dudley
1533 - 1553
Beheaded
No Issue
Died under House Arrest

Lady Katherine Grey
1540 - 1568
m 1560

Many years under House
Arrest Edward Seymour
1st Earl of Hertford
1538 - 1621

Lady Mary Grey
1545 - 1578
m 1555
Arrest

Thomas Keyes
Palace Gate Keeper
Died in Prison
1525 - 1571
No Issue

Ferdinando Strange
5th Earl of Derby
1559 - 1594
m 1583 Alice Spencer
1556 - 1637

William Stanley
6th Earl of Derby, King of Man
1561 - 1626
m 1594 Elizabeth de Vere
1575 - 1626

Edward Lord Beauchamp
1561 - 1612
m 1585 Honora Rogers
- after 1608

Lady Frances Stanley
1583 - 1635
m 1602 John Egerton
1st Earl of Bridgwater
1579 - 1649

James Stanley
7th Earl of Derby
1607 - 1651
Beheaded
m 1626 Charlotte de la Trémouille
1599 - 1663

William Seymour
2nd Duke of Somerset
2nd Earl of Hertford
1589 - 1660
m 1st 1610
Arabella Stuart
1575 - 1615
Imprisoned in the Tower
of London where she died insane.
No Issue
m 2nd 1616
Lady Frances Devereux
1599 - 1674
Had Issue (see p.116)

John Egerton, 2nd Earl of Bridgwater
1623 - 1686
m 1641 Lady Elizabeth Cavendish
1626 - 1663
Had Issue

Lady Amelia Sophia Stanley
1633 - 1703
m 1659
John Murray, 1st Marquess of Atholl
1631 - 1703
Had Issue

Descendants of Lady Frances Devereux to the present-day Prince of Wales

William Seymour, 2nd Duke of Somerset, 2nd Earl of Hertford
m Lady Frances Devereux

Lady Jane Seymour 1637 - 1679
m 1661 Charles Boyle, Viscount Dungarvan 1639 - 1694

Charles, 3rd Earl of Cork 1674 - 1703
m 1687 Juliana Noel 1701 - 1750

Richard, 4th Earl of Cork 1695 - 1753
m 1720 Lady Dorothy Savile 1699 - 1758

Lady Charlotte Elizabeth Boyle. Baroness Clifford 1731 - 1794
m 1748 William, 4th Duke of Devonshire 1720 - 1764

Lady Dorothy Cavendish 1750 - 1794
m 1766 William Henry Cavendish-Bentinck, 3rd Duke of Portland 1738 - 1809

Lt. Col. William Charles Cavendish-Bentinck 1780 - 1826
m 1816 Anne Wellesley 1788 - 1875

Rev. Charles William Frederick Cavendish-Bentinck 1817 - 1865
m 1859 Caroline Louise Burnaby 1833 - 1918

Nina Cecilia Cavendish-Bentinck 1862 - 1938
m 1881 Claude George, 14th Earl of Strathmore and Kinghorne 1855 - 1944

Lady Elizabeth Angela Marguerite Bowes Lyon 1900 -
m 1923 HRH George, Duke of York, later HM King George VI 1895 - 1952

HM Queen Elizabeth II 1926 -
m 1947 HRH Prince Phillip of Greece, Duke of Edinburgh 1921 -

HRH Charles, Prince of Wales 1949 -
m 1980 Lady Diana Frances Spencer 1961 -

Prince William of Wales 1981 -

Prince Henry of Wales 1984 -

Descendants of Lady Frances Devereux to the present-day Princess of Wales

William Seymour, 2nd Duke of Somerset, 2nd Earl of Hertford
m Lady Frances Devereux
|

Lady Mary Seymour   - 1673
m 1649 Heneage Finch, 3rd Earl of Winchilsea 1627 - 1659
|

Lady Frances Finch 1650 - 1712
m 1672 Thomas Thynne, 1st Viscount Weymouth 1640 - 1714
|

Frances Thynne 1673 - 1750
m 1690 Sir Robert Worsley of Appuldercombe, Bart. 1669 - 1747
|

Frances Worsley 1693 - 1736
m 1710 John Carteret, 1st Earl Granville 1690 - 1763
|

Lady Georgina Carolina Carteret   - 1780
m 1733 Hon. John Spencer of Althorp 1708 - 1746
|

John, 1st Earl Spencer 1734 - 1783
m 1755 Margaret Georgiana Poyntz 1737 - 1814
|

George John, 2nd Earl Spencer 1758 - 1834
m 1781 Lady Lavinia Bingham 1762 - 1831

Frederick, 4th Earl Spencer 1798 - 1857
m 1854 Adelaide Horatia Seymour 1825 - 1877

Charles Robert, 6th Earl Spencer 1857 - 1922
m 1887 Hon. Margaret Baring 1868 - 1906

Albert Edward, 7th Earl Spencer 1892 - 1975
m 1919 Lady Cynthia Hamilton 1897 - 1972

Edward John 8th Earl Spencer 1924 -
m 1954 Frances Ruth Burke Roche 1936 -

Diana Frances Spencer 1961 -
m 1980 HRH Charles, Prince of Wales 1948 -

Prince William of Wales 1981 -

Prince Henry of Wales 1984 -

Appendix

To avoid any confusion in the mind of the reader concerning valid and invalid marriage, annulment, engagement, proxy marriage, infant marriage, separation, perhaps the following might be helpful.

In that early half of the sixteenth century, with which we are concerned, England was a Catholic country, owing spiritual allegiance to the Pope. That authority was not questioned. There was no civil marriage, and the church, not the state, settled any matrimonial problems that might arise. The church held that the indissolubility of marriage was God's law, not a law of the church. The responsibility of the church was to interpret and operate that law. In essence it was a simple system. To be valid a marriage had to be before a priest and two witnesses and be consummated and it was no marrige if these conditions had not been complied with, and so an annulment was automatic.

It was also possible to obtain an annulment when the conditions for a valid marriage had not been complied with as when:
1. One partner had been forced into the marriage and had not given free consent to the union.
2. Consanguinity of the partners existed, either known or unknown.
3. The marriage remained unconsummated for a physical reason or for wilful reason.
4. One of the partners was already married.

A bodily separation of the couple (not a divorce) was granted for a serious reason involving danger to the physical or mental health of one of the partners caused by the other's mental disorder, a vice or a perversion.

The proxy marriage (sometimes called an engagement) was used chiefly by royalty when extensive dowry negotiations had to be carried out and when travelling was difficult and even dangerous - perhaps a bride had to cross several countries without adequate protection and risked violence and seizure. There had to be two proxy marriages - one in each country -and then a final ceremony with both partners present. Occasionally, quarrelsome families withdrew from the arrangement after the proxy marriages had been performed, but this was not a grave issue as no consummation had taken place. The proxy system was frequently abused, and caused endless political and other difficulties.

Then there was the custom of infant marriages. For reasons usually political, parents would arrange a proxy marriage for an infant child to another infant or even an adult but both had to reach puberty before they could come together. This was a very unhealthy custom, which led to much cruelty and distress.

The basic teaching, "Till death do us part," was accepted and adhered to by common folk, the small middle class and the minor aristocracy. There was the same law for prince and peasant, but the powerful (royalty and important nobles) tried all kinds of ruses to secure an annulment of a "marriage" which had become politically or personally inconvenient. Force was also used by some monarchs against bishops and popes and this was sometimes successful.

Charles Suffolk had had four marriages and three wives and Mary Suffolk three marriages and two husbands but if these are traced through there is no doubt that the Suffolk marriage was valid.

The marriage of Henry and Katherine was more complicated. Katherine, being Henry's brother's widow could not marry the king according to the law of the time but the Pope gave a dispensation for this to take place in spite of her wish not to marry again in England. As it happened, the dispensation was not necessary, for Arthur was a sickly boy who, although he had spent three nights in Katherine's bed, had not consummated their union. During her trial, the queen in open court stated that she had come to Henry a virgin and challenged the king to deny it. Henry gave no answer. A few years later he gave himself a divorce. Later still he overcame obstacles to his obsession by decapitating two wives and so making himself twice a widower.

End Notes

1. Agnes Strickland, *Lives of the Queens of England from the Norman Conquest.* Longman 1858. Reprinted by Cedric Chivers, Bath 1972: Vol. 2, p.94.

2. Agnes Strickland, *Lives of the Tudor and Stuart Princesses.* George Bell and Sons, London, 1888.

3. Agnes Strickland, *Lives of the Tudor and Stuart Princesses*, p.13.

4. Mary Anne Everett (Wood) Green, *Lives of the Princesses of England from the Norman Conquest.* Longman, 1849-55, p.53.

5. Mary Anne Everett (Wood) Green, p.39.

6. Mary Anne Everett (Wood) Green, p.71.

7. Agnes Strickland, *Lives of the Tudor and Stuart Princesses*, p.43.

8. Mary Anne Everett (Wood) Green, p.77.

9. Mary Anne Everett (Wood) Green, pp. 81, 82.

10. Agnes Strickland, *Lives of the Tudor and Stuart Princesses*, p.31.

11. Agnes Strickland, *Lives of the Tudor and Stuart Princesses*, p.33.

12. Agnes Strickland, *Lives of the Tudor and Stuart Princesses*, p.38.

13. Agnes Strickland, *Lives of the Tudor and Stuart Princesses*, p.31.

14. Agnes Strickland, *Lives of the Tudor and Stuart Princesses*, pp. 43 and 44.

15. Walter C. Richardson, *Mary Tudor, The White Queen.* Peter Owen, London. 1970, p.175.

16. Agnes Strickland, *Lives of the Queens of England from the Norman Conquest.* Vol.2, pp. 531 and 532.

17. Agnes Strickland, *Lives of the Queens of England from the Norman Conquest.* Vol. 2, p.536.

18. Agnes Strickland, *Lives of the Tudor and Stuart Princesses,* p.56.

19. Agnes Strickland, *Lives of the Queens of England from the Norman Conquest.* Vol. 2, p.548.

Bibliography

Burke's Peerage and Baronetage. Burke's Peerage Ltd. 1970.

Complete Peerage. St. Catherine's Press, London, 1926.

Debrett's Peerage and Baronetage. Macmillan, 1985.

Dictionary of National Biography.

Saint Mary's, Bury St. Edmunds. Guide.

Suffolk Garland or a Collection of Poems, Songs, Tales etc. Relative to that County. J. Row, Ipswich, 1818.

Auton, Jean. *Chroniques de Louis XII.* Renouard, 1889.

Bridge, John. *History of France from the Death of Louis XI.* Clarendon Press, 1921.

Brook, Roy. *The Story of Eltham Palace.* George Harrap & Co., 1960.

Brown, Mary Croom. *Mary Tudor, Queen of France.* Methuen, 1911.

Buchanan, Patricia. *Margaret Tudor, Queen of Scots.* Scottish Academic Press, 1985.

Burke, S. *Historical Portraits of the Tudor Dynasty and the Reformation Period.* John Hodges, 1879.

Bush, Mrs. Forbes. *Queens of France.* 1879.

Busch, Wilhelm. *England unter den Tudors.* Trans. A. Todd. A.D. Innes & Co., 1895.

Carmelianus, Petrus. *Solemn Ceremonies of the Betrothal and Marriage of the King's daughter, the Lady Mary, to the Prince of Castile, Archduke of Austria* (1508), Trans. James Gairdner. Camden Society, 1893.

Chapman, Hester. *The Sisters of Henry VIII.* Jonathan Cape, 1969.

Cocheris, H. *Entrée de Marie d'Angleterre, Femme de Louis XII à Abbeville et à Paris*. Paris, 1859.

Evans, Joan. *Magical Jewels of the Middle Ages and the Renaissance*. Clarendon Press, 1922.

Furnivall, E. *Manners and Meals in Olden Times*. Oxford University Press, 1868 and 1931.

Gairdner James. *Henry the Seventh*. Macmillan & Co, 1889.

Green, Mrs. Mary Anne Everett. *Lives of the Princesses of England*. Vol. 5, Longman, 1957.

Holinshed, Raphael. *Chronicle* (1577). edit. H. Ellis, 1807.

Louandre, F. *Histoire d'Abbeville*. Joubert, 1844.

Mackie, J. *The Earlier Tudors* (1485-1558) Vol. 7. Oxford History of England. Clarendon Press, 1952.

Marie d'Angleterre, Reine de France. *Lettres*. Conservées à la Bibliothèque Nationale. Publicées au 19 ième siecle. (Pre and post marriage correspondence from Mary to Louis).

Maulde La Clavière, Marie Alphonse de. *Histoire de Louis XII*. E. Leroux, 1889.

McKee, Alexander. *How We Found the MARY ROSE*. Souvenir Press Ltd., 1982.

Morpurgo, J. *Life Under the Tudors*. Peregrine Press, 1950.

Pardoe, Julia. *The Court and Reign of Francis the First*. Bentley, 1849.

Richardson, W.C. *Mary Tudor, The White Queen*. Peter Owen Ltd., 1970.

Rough, E.M.G. *Lady Margaret Beaufort*. Humphrey Milford, London, 1924.

Rule, Dr. Margaret. *The Mary Rose*. Conway Maritime Press, 1982.

Salter, Emma Gurney. *Tudor England Through Venetian Eyes,* William and Norgate, London, 1930.

Ford, Francis. *State Procession and Funeral of Mary, the ffrenche Quene from Westhorpe to St. Edmund's Monastery and Burial.* E.L. Barker, Bury St. Edmunds, 1882.

Strickland, Agnes. *Lives of the Queens of England from the Norman Conquest.* Longman, 1858; Chivers, 1972.

Strickland, Agnes. *Lives of the Tudor and Stuart Princesses.* Longman, 1868.

Thornton-Cook, Elsie. *Royal Marys: Princess Mary and Her Predecessors.* J. Murray & Co., London, 1929.

Tyler, Royall. *The Emperor Charles the Fifth.* Allen & Unwin, 1956.

Williams, Neville. *The Royal Residences of Great Britain.* Barrie & Rockcliff, London, 1960.

Woodward, Ida. *Five English Consorts of Foreign Princes.* Methuen & Co., London, 1911.

Wormald, Francis. *The Solemn Entry of Mary Tudor to Montreuil-sur-Mer in 1514.* Ed. J. Conway Davies. Oxford University Press, 1957.

Facsimile of the signature of "Mary the French Quene".

Acknowledgements

The author and the publisher wish to acknowledge with thanks the assistance of Lt. Cdr. Peter Whitlock of the Mary Rose Trust. They are also grateful to the fellows of Magdalen College, Cambridge for permission to use the photograph of the MARY ROSE on the cover of the book, and to the Marquess of Tavistock and the Trustees of the Bedford Estates for kind permission to reprint the portrait of Princess Mary and the Duke of Suffolk. The cover portrait of the Princess Mary is by courtesy of the UCAD-Photo service, Paris. The portrait of the Princess Mary and the Duke of Suffolk is reproduced by courtesy of the Hulton Picture Library.